CHEQUERED CHANCES

A Portrait of Lady Luxborough

Barrells Park. Drawing by James Saunders, c.1810.

CHEQUERED CHANCES

A Portrait of Lady Luxborough

A u d r e y   D u g g a n

BREWIN BOOKS

First published by
Brewin Books Ltd, 56 Alcester Road,
Studley, Warwickshire B80 7LG in 2008
www.brewinbooks.com

ISBN: 978-1-85858-290-0

A Cataloguing in Publication Record
for this title is available from the British Library

Typeset in Baskerville
Printed in Great Britain by
The Alden Press

CONTENTS

ACKNOWLEDGEMENTS

I would like to thank staff at the British Library, The National Portrait Gallery, the City of Westminster Archives, Wandsworth Local History Archives and the Public Records Office at Kew. Also staff at the Courtauld Institute of Art, London and the National Gallery.

I must thank Patrick Baird and his staff at the Local Studies and History Department and staff of the Arts, Language and Literature Department of Birmingham Central Library. Also staff at the Shakespeare Birthplace Trust, Stratford-upon-Avon; Warwick Library Local History Department; Warwickshire County Record Office and Tracey Williams at Solihull Heritage and Local Studies.

Thanks are also due to all at Lydiard House; to Sarah Finch-Crisp for permission to photograph portraits of Henrietta and her family and to Swindon Borough Council. To Arthur Carden and Canon Brian Carne for their help and advice. The former for allowing me to use a copy of his photograph of Barrells' double oak and portraits of the young and mature Robert Knight, Henrietta's husband. The latter as editor of *Report* in which has appeared abridged versions of my chapters concerning Lady Luxborough's poetry and letters. Also on this account acknowledgements are due to the editorial committee of the *Birmingham Historian*.

I would like to thank family members: Mrs Nancy Salford and Mrs D F Johnson for kind permission to use portraits of Henry Bolingbroke as a young man and Henrietta's son and daughter, the Honourable Henry and Henrietta Knight. Then I must not forget to thank Mr and Mrs John Craythorne for their permission to use a diagram of the layout of Henrietta's garden from their son's book, *Barrells Hall; From Riches to Ruins*.

I wish to say a special thank you to my friend and colleague, Jean Holland, who has word processed and amended the manuscript, and to my husband, Geoffrey, who has so tirelessly facilitated my research and contributed to much of it himself.

Finally, I want to thank my publisher, Alan, who has always been available to answer queries and Alistair who has offered invaluable advice over the photographs. Without such help and goodwill, this book would not have been brought to fruition.

INTRODUCTION

Henrietta, says William Sechel, was more "sinned against than sinning" – a comment which would seem to be a fair conclusion to draw. For the "scandal" of Lady Luxborough as she became was not so much her own, possibly naïve behaviour, but her punishment which was to last a lifetime.

What follows is the story of a talented and beautiful woman whose husband felt sufficiently betrayed to lock her away upstairs in attic rooms – finally to "banish" her to a tumbledown farmhouse, Barrells Hall, in Warwickshire where she could be hidden away from London's "polite" society which earlier had been her playground.

Throughout, the authority of the eighteenth century husband is paramount, and serves to throw into sharp relief the courage of a woman ultimately able to make a new and successful life for herself as a literary hostess of some distinction. One who with the aid of her close friend the poet, William Shenstone, was able to create a memorable garden and turn her house into an elegant dwelling.

A companion volume to my earlier book, *The World of William Shenstone, Chequered Chances* is a title taken from Henrietta's own words, depicting shades of joy and sadness. For this is how she came to view her life, and in consequence I have allowed Lady Luxborough whenever possible, through her letters to speak for herself. I have kept her original spelling save for the early "f" which frequently doubles as "s" and which makes understanding what she has to say more difficult. This means that down the centuries her voice is still clearly heard. We join with her in laughter as well as tears and in the end her transgression, real or imaginary, becomes of less consequence than the woman she turned out to be.

Chapter 1

BIRTH AND BACKGROUND

Henrietta St John was born on July 15, Saint Swithun's Day, a fact which we know to be true because, years later, in a letter to her great friend, William Shenstone, she says so. But there has been controversy surrounding where and when. Received opinion would have us believe that she was born at Lydiard House in Wiltshire, the family's country estate – a belief now known to be untrue. Instead, it is more likely that she was born in London at the St John's Berkley Street home. As for her exact date of birth, records[1] show that she was born "around 1699" although, surprisingly, there is no mention of a christening. It is a puzzle which prefigures uncertainties throughout Henrietta's life; one which like the sea, is going to turn out to be reluctant to yield up its secrets.

Henrietta was the daughter of Henry, Viscount St John, and his second wife Angelica Magdalene Wharton, a young widow whose very name proclaimed her piety. Here it is helpful to remember that Henry was a family name which can cause problems if the father, "Old Frumps" as he was not very affectionately called by his family, is confused with his son, also Henry, later to become Lord Bolingbroke.

Viscount St John had first married Lady Mary Rich who died giving birth to Henrietta's famous half-brother Henry, in 1678. Known as Harry to his friends, this was the man who was to play an important role in his young sister's story. He was twenty-one when she was born and quick to realise that Herriot as he affectionately called her, was no ordinary child. He it was who took an active role in her education, supervising her reading and advising upon, some might say meddling, in her social life and marriage prospects. The two were to grow extremely fond of each other and throughout their lives corresponded regularly.

That Bolingbroke was one of the most brilliant men of his age, there can be little doubt. A Member of Parliament at twenty-three, his meteoric rise to cabinet rank was to find him, as Foreign Secretary in 1713, the principal negotiator of the Treaty of Utrecht; and decades later, his *Idea of a Patriot King*, published in 1738, was to lay the foundation stone of nineteenth century Toryism. A friend of Pope, he had entré into the homes of many of the best-known writers of the day. At Court, in Parliament and at the most exclusive of London clubs his name was a by-word. Just such a man, one might feel, to be a suitable mentor for his young sister.

Perhaps he was – or possibly not; for he was a man who epitomized the double standards of the time. He was promiscuous. He was sexually voracious and a regular client of Sally Salisbury who worked at a Covent Garden brothel run by Mother Wisebourne. This was a woman who procured her staff by posing with her Bible as a prison visitor, a ploy which enabled her to arrange the "freedom" of likely girls, some little more than children. Also on her books was the famous Lord Chesterfield who, according to Frank Harris, liked to have "his eyelids licked by two naked whores"[2]. At this time, there were over a hundred brothels in Covent Garden, and the running of them, although lucrative, was a risky business. Mother Needham who had run a nearby establishment, died a dreadful death in the pillory which, for three days, had been her prison.

Bolingbroke's debauched private life was well known. As a young man he had contracted syphilis and when "out on the town", his frequent drinking bouts involved him in numerous brawls. Understood in this context, a line from one of Swift's poems is not so outrageous after all. References to the great man's "drinking like a fish and f... like a goat"[3], were all too true.

In the eighteenth century a number of men behaved in this way, but well-born women were expected to be chaste although there were exceptions. Men had to be sure that their heirs were legitimate, of the same bloodline, and so kept their wives in check. It was a belief summed up in Dr Johnson's, "The chastity of women is all important as all property depends upon it"[4], and one which held, as poor Henrietta was to discover, that any departure from the stony path of virtue, either real or imaginary would result in dire consequences.

But to return to the baby, Henrietta. What is known of her young childhood? Sadly little. She spent, during her early years, much time at Battersea Manor on the Thames, with frequent visits to Lydiard House, or to one of their town houses in London. The family was rich and owned numerous properties acquired by means of judicious marriage contracts, which ensured that the little girl's formative years were lived in luxury.

By modern standards all three of these properties were enormous; especially Battersea Manor which boasted forty rooms on each floor. The oldest part of the house dated from the fourteenth century, but over the years this had been extensively added to by a variety of different owners. In 1627, the then owner, Lord Grandison, had added the Jacobean wing which was where Henrietta's family now lived. It must have been an impressive building – its lofty ceilings decorated with "delicate strap-work plaster", and its walls lighted by many windows. A feature of this wing of the house was a lovely downstairs "Roame wainsitted with ceadar"[5] built from the wood of many magnificent cedars which adorned the park. Here, when fires were lit and the wood warmed to a reddish glow, one glimpses a degree of comfort although the overall impression is of cold and draught, for the house faced northeast and took the brunt of winter gales that swept up the Thames. The servants fared even worse. Their quarters were to be found in the oldest part of the house, comprising a warren of small, dark and rat infested rooms. These were reached by means of "parlours, dyning rooms, chambers, closets, galleries, buttereys, pantries, kitchens and larders"[6], all of which presented a picture of indescribable dirt, darkness and drear.

The park belonging to the manor was a different story. There, fringed by a shady lime walk and terminating in a low, terrace type wall, were wide lawns which ran down to the river's edge – the busiest waterway in Britain with sights and sounds providing an ever changing panorama. It was from here that the little Henrietta would have watched the boats. The ferry boats that plied their passage to and from Chelsea on the other side of the river where the spire of its little church could be seen on the skyline. The skilled watermen who river raced their small crafts to and from the city and barges loaded with produce, some belonging to rich merchants with ornate and gilded carvings on their prow. On state occasions, she would even have seen the royal barge, that Rolls Royce of the river, splendiferous with its complement of colourful courtiers, liveried servants and panoply of unfurled flags as it sped upstream to Westminster.

Far removed from the sights and sounds of the great river, the child also spent time at Lydiard and here there hangs a portrait of her, painted when she was two years old. It is a painting which offers a foretaste of the woman that Henrietta was to become, a child with a crown of luxuriant dark hair, an expression that is curiously "knowing", and wide, black eyes uncannily perceptive. As a young woman, Henrietta was to be renowned for her "bush" of black hair, and in her maturity her perceptions were to be sharpened upon a whetstone of pain. But that is in the future. For the present it is to Battersea that the narrative returns.

At Battersea where she grew up, and where she spent a greater part of her time, the little girl lived with her parents and grand parents, the exemplary Sir Walter St John and his wife, Johanna. This was a couple who epitomized so much that was good in those dying days of the feudal Lord of the Manor and his Lady. Together they did much to improve the well being of their community, leading the congregation at prayer in the village church of St Mary's and supervising the building of a new school for the village children which they endowed with their own money. Lady St John was also a keen gardener and spent much time and expense in beautifying the estates of both Battersea and Lydiard. Perhaps this love of gardening was in the family genes, for it was a pastime to be enthusiastically embraced by her granddaughter when in the future she was to become mistress of Barrells, a farmhouse near Henley-in-Arden, in Warwickshire.

Not all Henrietta's relations were so worthy. Certainly not her father, Viscount St John who, in 1684, had been involved in a drunken brawl at the Globe Tavern in Shoe Lane, killing Sir Edward Estcourt, a man whose only claim to fame would seem to have been his unfortunate death.

Found guilty of murder, and sentenced to be hanged at Tyburn, an experience which, not surprisingly, terrified him, Lord St John fled for a time to France, leaving his six year old son, Henry, in the charge of his grandparents. In order to obtain a "reprieve" he had been obliged to pay Charles II a substantial bribe of £16,000. A gesture which lightened the coffers but did little to improve his reputation. He was safer out of the way. His absence had repercussions, as even a "bad" father is better than no father at all. In an attempt to counter the influence of the runaway, the grandparents subjected their young charge to a harsh regime of study, especially religious studies, which served only to turn the child away from those very virtues they were trying so desperately to inculcate. Perhaps this is where Harry Bolingbroke's problems, if problems they were, first began.

Apart from Bolingbroke, Henrietta had three other brothers. First there was George and later John (Jack) St John who was to prove peculiarly unpleasant when, in the future, his sister most needed support. Even so, she seems to have been fond of him and when he died in 1749, became physically ill with shock and grief. Then there was Hollis; a young man who returned her affection and about whom, apart from the fact that he was overweight and unable or unwilling to apply himself to very much, little is known. Except that he died young, at the early age of thirty-two, leaving his sister some family jewels and money in his will.

There are also the ancestors. Behind a curtain of years is to be found Lady Castlemaine, Henrietta's great aunt and notorious mistress of Charles II by whom she had a son, the Duke of Grafton. There is worse. Henrietta's uncle, John Wilmot, the dissipated second Earl of Rochester, had drunk himself to death before his niece was born. He was a favourite at the Court of Charles II, a wit and a considerable poet as the final stanza of his delightful little song, "Love and Life" demonstrates. In lines evocative of some of the later poetry of John Donne he begs his mistress:

Then talk not of inconstancy
False hearts and broken vows
If I by miracle can be
This live long minute true to thee
'Twas all that Heav'n allows [7].

In other words, enjoy the present and do not worry about commitment! All rather "modern" one might think. Rochester was thirty-two when he died of drink and disease – a broken man, his life summed up in another of his own verses:

All my past life is mine no more
The flying hours are gone
Like transitory Dreams giv'n o,er
Where Images are kept in store
By memory alone [8].

So, from a bran tub of relatives and ancestors might the list continue, but the point is already made – that in all families, whether renowned like Henrietta's or more ordinary; the good, the bad, and the plain indifferent all share the same stage. The fact that the St Johns were aristocrats with an ancestry that dated back hundreds of years, made not one whit of difference. Except perhaps, for the publicity that they were able to engineer for themselves in the little churches which nestled within the skirts of those two manor houses where they chose to live.

At Lydiard, the visitor has many notable monuments to see including, above the high altar, a genealogical table of what purports to be the entire St John family in its many and varied ramifications. At Battersea, the little church of St Mary's was to be rebuilt soon after Henrietta's death. However, the famous east window which also celebrates the ancestry of the St Johns, was preserved from the earlier building, its design incorporating the coats of arms of Henry VII, Margaret Beauchamp, and Queen Elizabeth I, each with a portrait medallion below, demonstrating how closely down the centuries the family had become established in royal and aristocratic circles.

When Henrietta was born, the village of Battersea not only had its church and manor house, but its own public house, The Raven, which faced the village green. The green boasted a water pump where women queued for water with their buckets and where in summer, under the shade of tall cedars, the villagers would congregate. It was here, in scenes redolent of Blake's "The Echoeing Green" [9], that the men would smoke their pipes and "laugh away care"; that their women folk would bring domestic chores outside while the children whose "sports shall be seen" would gambol and play within sight of a clutch of thatched cottages where they lived.

Not all was so idyllic. Close by the lavender scented garden of the manor and the near-by glow of St Mary's east window at sunset, were tidal marshes – stark wasteland of Dickensian proportions which robbers and vagabonds had made their own. Because of this, the St Johns were unlikely to have frequented an adjacent lane, "Ye footpath to London" [10], for fear of foot pads. It would have been safer and easier to travel up river by boat or if on land, by coach with an armed footman on board, to the capital.

None of this would have concerned the little Henrietta; privileged, favoured and aristocratic – cocooned within a world programmed to protect her, so long as she played by the rules. That allegedly she did not and in consequence was obliged to suffer, is her own sad story. One with its origins already glimpsed, perhaps in that Lydiard portrait – of a child mature and beautiful beyond her years. One who was destined to plough a lonely furrow.

Chapter 2

THE YOUNG HENRIETTA

In the early eighteenth century, the education of little girls was rudimentary. Rather they were trained to find, or to have found for them, a suitable husband who would expect them "to be passive, maternal, submissive, modest, docile and virtuous"[1]. They would expect to have little influence over their children and none at all in any sphere other than the household where ultimately they were still subject to their husband's authority. It was current thinking that women were inferior to men, "children of a larger growth"[2], and like children must be guided and disciplined when necessary. Dr Johnson's famous retort, that "a young woman's preaching is like a dog's walking on his hinder legs"[3] reflected this, and one wonders how he would have reacted to the ordination of women priests – or worse, women bishops!

Even so, until approaching womanhood when the first tongues began to wag, the young Henrietta would have led a charmed life. She would have learnt to read with the aid of a hornbook, an elementary primer, consisting of pages of upper and lower case letters framed within a "window" of cattle horn. From her earliest years she would have practised her embroidery on fabric stretched across a frame, designed to facilitate the manipulation of her needle. It was a skill that encouraged the choosing and matching of colours and one which would stand her in good stead as an adult, when she was obliged to refurbish her home at Barrells. She would have taken music lessons on the spinet, a small early keyboard instrument. One to which Mrs Delaney, a contemporary of Henrietta's, advised all young girls to "stick close". It would be exciting to think that she was taught by "the great Mr Handel", a musician whose friendship she was privileged, years later, to enjoy. But there is no evidence for this, and in any case, because of his many commitments, it is likely that his teaching would have been restricted to members of the royal household – a duty that he was obliged to fulfil.

Another sure, enjoyable and accepted way of acquiring general knowledge, was by means of table games, those early precursors of our "Ludo" and "Snakes and Ladders". By flickering candlelight on dark winter evenings, the little Henrietta would have spun her Tee-To-Tum (sic) and moved her marker accordingly. She would have learnt her basic geography from games which consisted of a map painted upon a board with a sectioned, numbered track that snaked round to places and countries of interest. Historical games followed the same pattern but featured instead the kings and queens of England.

She would also have played instructional games, which taught good manners, or games of moral improvement. The latter would have promoted the virtue of bravery or hard work and pilloried the vices of jealousy and sloth. A few years later this was achieved by means of a rule book which provided a verse for each of the sectioned spaces containing pictures of "good" and "bad" children. Take, as an example, "Idle Jane":

Now pray is not Jane a true emblem of sloth
See! how idle she lolls in her chair
She still must remain in the seat where she is
'Till the Totam's spun twice by each play'r [4].

But Henrietta was far from dependent upon board games alone. She had an excellent French governess, Mlle Haille, "The best creature in the world... full of mildness, modesty and good sense". A young woman who "has honour enough to make a very valuable man" [5]; praise indeed! One who had perception enough to encourage her young charge in the reading she so enjoyed. Henrietta's education was also supervised by Bolingbroke who, as has been seen, was a brilliant if unscrupulous man. He recognized the child's potential and was happy to guide her in her studies which included English, French and later, Italian literature, although he laughingly dissuaded her from embarking upon a course of philosophy.

There were also exciting social diversions. One of these was "Powell's Famous Puppet Show", in which "Punch fought with a pig in burlesque". The event is recorded by Mrs Delaney (née Mary Granville) in her autobiography, who adds that a member of the party was "My Lord Bolingbroke... (who) made me sit upon his lap to watch it" [6]. There is no mention of Henrietta, but surely she must have been there, watching the slapstick magic of Mr Punch as he bashed and banged his way through the story.

Mary Granville, as she was then, was born in the same year as Henrietta – in 1699. Thomas Powell's Puppet Theatre operated from circa 1710–1712, so the children in the party would have been between eleven and thirteen. Rather old to sit upon an adult's knee one would have thought, but perhaps today's preoccupation with political correctness taints one's perception.

Another amusement which occupied young women was the sending of "Bout Rimes" to each other. These consisted of a quatrain of doggerel verse with the end rhyme to be supplied by the recipient. As the lines below make clear, the challenge to supply the missing words was not difficult:

> *When friendship such as yours our hours* **bless**
> *It soothes our cares and makes affliction* **less**
> *Opprest by woes, from you I'm sure to* **find**
> *A sovereign cure for my distempered* **mind** [7].

Later, Henrietta attended masquerades, those boisterous and popular gatherings across the river at Chelsea, at Ranelagh or Vauxhall Gardens; functions at which a carnival atmosphere prevailed, dancing and disguise providing a heady mix of mystery, romance and opportunities for flirting. She would also have enjoyed more decorous affairs, balls where the minuet still held sway and she danced until dawn. Henrietta's great friend Frances, Countess of Hertford, recalls these youthful escapades with affection:

> *No Walk was long enough or Exercise painful enough to hurt us, as we childishly imagined. Yet after a Ball or Masquerade, have we not come home well contented to pull off our ornaments and fine cloaths in order to go to rest* [8]. *(sic)*

Years later, this same friend was to extol her warm hearted Henrietta as a woman whose letters were "more agreeable and entertaining" than those of other friends because they demonstrate "more of friendship than any Body's else (sic) have the Art of doing" [9].

Before her marriage Henrietta was invited to fashionable assemblies at the homes of the great, the good and possibly the not so good. Homes like Montague House in Bloomsbury where guests were routinely entertained to concerts and Handel frequently played. Then there were card parties for the celebration of ombre – an eighteenth century card game which originated from Spain and was not unlike our modern whist. It was immortalized by Pope in his "The Rape of the Lock", a poem in which the players are viewed as military combatants – the card table, in disarray, as a battlefield:

> *Clubs, Diamonds, Hearts in wild disorder seen*
> *With throngs promiscuous strow the level green* [10].

The game was played with a pack of forty cards. This included aces in the guise of matadors, kings with "forky beards", queens with flowers in their hands and, representing the commonality, knaves with caps on their heads and holding halberds. There were tea parties and drives in the park. There were visits to the opera, a field that was to become dominated by Handel whose "Il Pastor Fido", staged in 1712, Henrietta much admired. There was Gay's "Beggar's Opera" with its medley of folk songs and subtle truisms:

> *"The fly that sips treacle is lost in the sweets"* [11],

a show which drew large crowds and one which Henrietta must have seen because she knew Gay as a friend and admired his wit. There were visits to play houses where Shakespeare, in the eighteenth century, was not always well received, but Vanbrugh's "Relapse" and Susannah Centrilivre's "The Busybody", were! Life was lived at a gallop – its flavour encapsulated in Pope's, "...opera, park, assembly, play" [12], a line which points with his customary precision to the social merry-go-round upon which all young, marriageable women of the upper classes were obliged to jump.

If Frances Hertford could commend Henrietta for her letter writing, it was her punctiliousness that impressed her brother. She always answered his letters promptly – even from Bath where she was staying in 1722 and the routine, both medical and social, was rigorous. It was a time when ladies' fashions were "fantastic enough in all conscience" [13], a comment to which the Duchess of Montague, a guest at the same time, gives credence:

> *Their hair is short, as curled as Cab's powdered white as snow, with yellow coarse flourished gauze ruffled round their head (and) they are rouged like scarlet cloth* [14].

So was Henrietta kept busy as a glimpse at her social calendar makes clear. In spring and autumn she was frequently at (the) Bath. In the summer, at Lydiard "in the midst of country jollity" [15]. By late summer it was time to return to one of the family's London town houses for The Season, and what remained of the rest of the year was spent at Battersea. It was a peripatetic social round, a panorama of different settings with some new faces for good measure, thrown in at each.

One of the highlights in Henrietta's young life occurred in 1719 when she was presented at Court, an occasion for which she wore a magnificent gown made out of material that was a present from the Marquise, Marie Claire. This lady who was anxious to establish friendship with Henrietta, was her brother Harry's mistress, soon to become his wife. Writing from France where the two were living in a relationship which seems to have been accepted by the St John family, the Marquise tells of her pleasure in being allowed to provide, not only material for a gown, but if necessary, subsequent trimmings to adorn it. Such overtures were a success. Upon a subsequent visit by Marie Claire to London when she came on her husband's behalf to lobby support for a possible return to England, the two women – much to Bolingbroke's delight – became firm friends. By all accounts, Henrietta's gown was much admired, if that is measured by the number of young men who showed an interest in her. It would have needed to be because competition was considerable. Mary Thynne, sister to Frances, Herriot's close friend, describes a Court function in 1715 and especially the jewels and gowns worn by those present. First there was my Lady Weymouth, whose gown was "gold embroidered with green, and green and gold small knots". Who wore "...diamond earrings and (a), pearl necklace. Whose finery contrasted with my Lady Carteret in her "blue satin, embroidered with gold... and blue and silver knots". The latter was a young woman who wore both her own and jewellery she had borrowed, which hints of how the girls helped each other: "her own diamond necklace and Lady Weymouth's cross, and a pair of three-dropped earrings borrowed of the jeweller...". Earrings of this type were fashionable, and so were jewelled crosses. Frances, herself, wore "three dropped earrings and a cross". Her gown was cherry and silver and she wore "a bunch of five diamonds in her hair" [16]. There can be little doubt that on these occasions young girls with high-sounding names were encouraged to dazzle and Henrietta would have been no exception. They also knew the value of money. Mary carefully lists the price of the material (stuff) from which each girl's gown was made. Three pounds a yard, four pounds, forty-seven shillings – all represent enormous expense. The stakes were high and these young aristocrats knew it!

One might have expected that the rest of the year, 1719, would have been happy for Henrietta but it was not. There was an unhappy love affair that possibly had its origins in that Court appearance to which Marie

Claire, had contributed with her generous present. There were hopes of a possible marriage, but these were dashed. Bolingbroke writes from France of his concerns. "A man of narrow fortune, a mean birth or a bad character shall never by my consent have you thrown away on him" [17]. Then, within a month, a reference to his sister's "Publick misfortunes", first introduces the possibility of "scandal". Who the man was, "how public" and what "misfortune", is not known. But her brother's plea that, instead, she should hurry up and marry suitably so as to present him with a nephew before he is too old, shows the family's concern that she was not yet married. And it would have distressed Henrietta. Affectionate and warm hearted, she would have found it difficult to distance herself from a suitor when inclination prompted otherwise.

In any case, her brother's anxieties and aspirations for his sister are to be placed in context. We should remember they were penned by the erstwhile lover of one of London's most expensive prostitutes, a Miss Gumley, who must have been a great deal more attractive than her name allows; and before that of Clara, an orange girl for whom as a young man, he penned the following lines:

> *Survey thyself, contemplate every grace*
> *Of that sweet form, of the angelic face*
> *Then Clara say, were these delicious charms*
> *Mean't for lewd brothels and ruffians' arms?* [18].

Then there was the delectable F...y, and so on. One thing is clear. In days past, Bolingbroke had been content to share Clara with "rude ruffians"; was an eager frequenter of "lewd brothels". Those were the days when, for him, the gutter and the crystal goblet held equal sway.

So much for the brother about whom there will be more later. For the sister things were to prove otherwise. The standard demanded of her must always be geared to the price she would fetch in the marriage market. As things turned out, hers was to be a marriage that did not take place for another eight years and by that time, it is arguable, she would have been ready to commit herself to more or less, anybody. Then she was of an age when most of her friends were married with several children. That is how things were, and until then, it is time to consider another aspect of Henrietta's life.

Chapter 3

FRIENDSHIP

Henrietta was outgoing, affectionate and warm-hearted. She was gregarious and likeable and made ample use, as did her friends, of the balls, masquerades, operas and theatres available to her in London and elsewhere.

However, to describe her in this way is really not to describe her at all. For there was another Henrietta, not so well known perhaps: a thoughtful, intelligent girl who enjoyed reading – in French and Italian as well as English – walking and sober discussion. One who relished the intellectual challenge of philosophy and most certainly did not fit into society's pedestrian slot, designed for the curtailment of such activities by women. This Henrietta is unlikely to have been known to many and especially not to her parents, for it was a side of her shown only to intimates. Friends like Frances, Countess of Hertford and Mrs Elizabeth Rowe, the Somerset poet. Friends with whom laughter, of which there was a great deal, sounded a different note. One not wholly frivolous.

By the time that Henrietta and Frances were in their teens they were already firm friends. Frances, as was frequently the custom at this time, had married early and by the tender age of sixteen was the mother of Lady Betty and living with her young husband in a rented house in Albemarle Street. It was a proximity of which both girls made ample use and one which laid the foundation for a life-long friendship.

That the two became inseparable is hardly surprising for they shared much in common. But later there were to be differences and one of the most important of these is to be found in the men that the two women married. As family letters testify, Frances' marriage was extremely happy. When her husband had been obliged to leave home for a while on business he writes to his bride in anticipation of "the so much longed for kiss". A comment that might give rise to some surprise as this was an arranged alliance.

Two years later, this same young husband was to assure his wife that "there was nothing under heaven but yourself that I love" [1]. It was a belief he retained until his death in 1750, three years after inheriting the family title from his detestable father, Lord Somerset.

During the whole of their life together the Hertfords, whenever separated and for whatever reason, wrote to each other every day. The contrast with many of the marriages contracted by the St Johns could not be more stark. Henrietta's brother Bolingbroke, also married a "suitable" girl chosen by the family – a union to which he was to refer as "...a trifling piece of news" and one which was to make no difference to his predilection for prostitutes. Nearly a decade later Henrietta was to marry Robert Knight, son of Robert Knight, senior, about whom there is to be more later. The son was also a doubtful man, and the point of all this is that Frances had a loving and supportive husband. Henrietta did not and never would have.

Elizabeth Rowe, the third in this triumvirate of friends, was a Somerset poet of considerable stature. Her *Poems on Several Occasions*, by *Philomena* as she called herself, had received much favourable comment and her eulogy to her late husband was so much admired by Pope that he included it as an appendix to the second edition of his own *Eloise and Abelard*. It was a grand gesture by the great man and one which brought her welcome publicity. Another of Mrs Rowe's admirers was the well known poet, Matthew Prior – as was Sir Isaac Watts the hymn writer; and it was not to be long before Frances' grandfather at Longleat took up her cause. Soon came invitations to Marlborough Castle, the Hertford's ancestral home in Wiltshire beside the river Kennet where Henrietta was always a welcome guest, which is how the friendship began.

At the time of her first meeting with Henrietta, Elizabeth Rowe was still coming to terms with her widowhood. Like the Hertford's, her marriage too had been idyllically happy. But unlike theirs it had been very brief. For five years only she had been married to a partner who, although fifteen years her junior, had died from consumption at the young age of thirty-five. It was a tragedy from which she never fully recovered, but one which brought her to Marlborough more frequently than if events had been different. It meant that her loss was Henrietta's gain and explains how the latter came to spend so much of her time, with not one, but two well read and intelligent women.

Elizabeth, already established in literary circles, was now living, as she had chosen, in retirement at Frome – her visits to Marlborough her only link with the wider world. Frances had a long life ahead. Her considerable achievements belonging to the future, she was supported and encouraged by her adoring husband, was already organizing literary gatherings at her London home. Not without humour it would seem. For according to the young Lady Winchelsee who was frequently present, it was at one of these functions that the Countess "engaged Mr Eusden to write upon a wood, enjoining him to mention no tree but the Aspen, and no flower but the King-cup"[2]. The "fun" lines below prove him to have been equal to the task, and possibly, to date the occasion at around 1717, the date of Lady Betty's birth – for the second stanza describes a young baby waking up.

> *Your Aspen tree to which he stood confined.*
> *Is but the Rattle to some peevish wind*
> *Which grave Dame Nature does forever shake*
> *To still the Zephyrs when they first awake*[3].

Later, the Countess was to become patron to James Thomson, author of *The Seasons,* which was to cause more than a ripple of excitement, some years later among Henrietta's Warwickshire Coterie. Frances also took up the cause of Stephen Duck, "the thresher poet", a country man like Robert Burns whose work she was to bring to the attention of the future Queen Caroline. Frances' interest in literature encouraged her to write poetry of her own and, in an age when letter writing was as much an art form as the short story today, wrote letters that were witty, enjoyable and perceptive. Henrietta also was to write poetry and as Shenstone later testifies, her letters, written with "abundant ease, politeness and vivacity", provide invaluable social commentary.

So were the three women admirably matched. They discussed poetry and literature; they went for long walks in Windsor Forest with poems in their pocket books and lines in their heads, with which to challenge one another. They read plays – played the spinet and the virginals and unlike today, were wholly reliant upon their own resources. They drank tea together and managed to create, however inadvertently, a parallel world to that of young men at university.

Their favourite English texts were Dryden, Spencer and Shakespeare; they also read Tasso together and Guarini's *Il Pastor Fido* in its original Italian. The Guarini was especially popular with Henrietta and one can see why. As the extract below demonstrates, it creates a perception of romantic love with a ready appeal to an impressionable and warm-hearted woman.

My sweetheart gently turned
Those dear and radiant
Eyes of hers – all beauty, all desire –
Toward me sparklingly and seemed to say
"Give me your heart,
for nothing else gives me life" [4].

Mrs Rowe had been guided in her studies by a greatly respected and well-known academic, Bishop Ken, as it is likely had Frances. Henrietta's education had been overseen by her brother, Bolingbroke, so together the three women would have made a formidable debating team.

Marlborough was to become a second home to Henrietta; but these long rambles in Windsor Forest were later to be remembered, not only with infinite pleasure but also pain. This was when Henrietta had married and was expected to spend much time in France where she was homesick for the England that she had left behind.

In the meantime there was much to enjoy around the estate where the novelty of the folly, the newly minted grotto and hermitage was current. In keeping with the times, the infamous Lady Vane was to build a grotto constructed entirely of seashells at a cost of five thousand pounds – an incredible amount of money and an undertaking much admired by William Shenstone as well it might have been! Both Pope, at his home at Twickenham, and the Queen at Richmond built hermitages and Lady Hertford too, in her castle grounds. No doubt it was an innocent enough frivolity, enabling the wealthy, amid much popular talk of shepherds and shepherdesses, hermits and hermitesses, to pretend that they were living like an idyllic peasantry. Years later when exiled at Barrells, Henrietta under Shenstone's guidance, was to borrow from these ideas which were to provide her with a blueprint for the future.

When they were apart, Frances and Henrietta wrote long letters to each other for fun, detailing their daily lives. Some of these were in doggerel rhyming couplets – others in a more conventional prose. But prose or rhyme they all demonstrate a genuine and warm affection. They tell of eager anticipation; of meetings in London, Battersea, Marlborough or St Leonards and it was surely a time that Henrietta would have wished to continue for ever. But things never do... and why in this instance, they were so abruptly and graphically ended, is to be recounted in the next chapter.

Chapter 4

MARRIAGE

Up until Henrietta's marriage and exile, the friendship of the women remained firm. Mrs Rowe, born in 1672 and the eldest of the three, was to die in 1737, but the love and affection between the Countess and Mrs Knight, as Henrietta was to become, continued (minus a sad interval brought about by the latter's "disgrace"), until Frances died in 1753.

The three devised pet names for each other. Elizabeth Rowe continued to use "Philomena", the name under which she had published her verse. Lady Hertford was "Renée" and Henrietta chose "Marion" – names which added piquancy to the long and fanciful rhyming letters they sent to each other and which shed some light upon the life style of young aristocratic women in Georgian England.

Written in 1722, a rhyming letter from Henrietta to Frances describes the latter's role as lady-in-waiting to Princess, later Queen Caroline. Although the position is privileged, it is also tiring and her duties not always pleasant. There is a constant crush of people with whom she is obliged to be civil and the Prince's jokes, frequently in poor taste, can present a problem. So it is that we see her subject to some discomfort and embarrassment,

> *...retired behind the Chair of State*
> *Where compelled to praise what you most hate;* [1]

These letters were dashed off with a frequency in keeping with the pace at which they lived. The following lines, written on 30 October 1726, and illustrating Henrietta's affection for her friend:

Marion's intent is only to express,
In lowly style her love and tenderness...

Are answered promptly the next day with a rejoinder from Frances in similar vein:

To bright Maria dearest of her friends
These few dull lines the faithful Renée sends.

It is a fond response in a letter which ends with the loving message:

News I have none, for 'twill be none to say
I love you more and better every day [2].

Perhaps it is worth pondering the style of these letters a moment. The tone is sentimental and today two young women would not communicate in this way, or if they did, a sexual motive might be presumed. This is clearly not the case here. In the eighteenth century, Henrietta and Frances expressed themselves in a fashionable way. Neither were they insincere. Perceptions change, and what we may view as contrived, they would have understood as innocent fun.

Later, in a more conventional prose letter, Henrietta was to confide in her friend of her own warm-heartedness. "Tis my heart guides my pen" [3], she admits; a revealing comment for, without doubt, it was the future Mrs Knight's warm heart that plunged her later into so much trouble, precipitating her husband's action which was to result in her exile.

We first hear of Robert Knight, the man Henrietta was to marry, in a letter from Henry Bolingbroke to his father in August 1720. What he says is complimentary. "I have not heard from Mr Knight", a young man who he describes as "a very pretty youth" [4], and enjoying himself in Paris. Indeed, Bolingbroke's approval of this young man would seem to be in inverse proportion to his disapproval of his sister's ill-starred suitor of the previous year (see Chapter 2). And there were reasons for this. Robert

Knight came from a socially acceptable Essex family even though his father, Robert Knight senior, cashier of the notorious South Sea Company at the time of its collapse, had absconded with a considerable illegal fortune to the continent. That he was aided in his flight by people of influence who should have been above such chicanery – the same who put a chartered ship at his disposal to facilitate his escape, did not matter either. Nor did the fact that a Royal Proclamation offered a reward of £2000 for his capture. More important than all this was that upon his arrival in Paris, Mr Knight was able to use his illegal money to buy La Planchette, an extravagantly magnificent estate, and live there in great style. Money mattered and concern about where it came from was secondary. This was a man who lived like a lord and who would be able, when the time came, to provide like one for any future daughter-in-law. A man who had bought status and whose son was Henry Bolingbroke's friend.

Perhaps, then, a romance with Henrietta was only a matter of time? Certainly it did take time, another seven years in fact before the two were safely married. And meanwhile Henrietta was to continue the merry-go-round that was her social calendar. In October 1723 she was again at Bath where, "the atmosphere is lively". In June of the following year she has been ill of a "feavour" and upon the advice of her physician has been "swallowing Jesuit's Bark". It was one of those fevers which became more frequent as she grew older, which by the time she was exiled in Warwickshire, were responsible for putting her to bed for days at a time.

Then came a most important event; the arrival in London in 1724, of Henrietta's new sister-in-law, the Marquise, Marie Claire. In an attempt to "buy" influence, she came at Bolingbroke's behest, bearing a bribe of £11,000 for George I's Mistress, the greedy Duchess of Kendal. Bolingbroke (see Chapter 11) had set his heart upon a return to England but for this to happen his civil rights had to be restored and his attainder repealed. As things stood this was unlikely to happen, but time had passed since his Jacobite meddling and it was hoped that the Duchess who wielded considerable influence with the King, could persuade him to change course.

Marie Claire was an exceedingly charming woman. She needed to be if her mission were to prove successful and she was soon to find that a longer stay in London than first anticipated was going to be necessary. She had arrived in May 1724, and was not to leave until November of that year which was ample time for her to get to know Henrietta well. At first she stayed with the St Johns in Albemarle Street where the two women struck up a warm friendship. Henrietta who was used to spending much time in France, spoke excellent French and it was not long before she was tutoring her new sister-in-law in English by means of regular lessons which were, amidst much laughter, thoroughly enjoyed by both. Then it was decided that Marie Claire should rent a small house of her own. It was to be near to the St Johns and when a property, also in Albemarle Street, came on the market, it was not long before Henrietta became involved in her removal plans. By aiding her in "ordering her house", which involved everything from choosing soft furnishings to hiring servants, it was a time when she soon began to feel as if she were moving herself.

This was a friendship that greatly pleased Bolingbroke. He had prepared the ground carefully for such an eventuality, as had Marie Claire herself, adding interesting and amusing postscripts to her husband's loving letters to his sister from Paris. Now she wrote to Paris from England, telling Bolingbroke how charmed she was with Henrietta and with the rest of the family too. Their joint influence would have carried much weight – and it is arguable that by now the couple had already fixed upon young Robert Knight, as a suitable husband for Henrietta. A girl whose social clock was ticking – she was already twenty-five – and one for whom marriage was now an imperative.

Henrietta was not to marry until 1727, but it is now worth considering the years that run up to this for any light that can be shed upon the courtship. In spite of the lack of recorded evidence, received opinion has always maintained that her marriage with Robert Knight was a love match; but if this were so, why did the courtship take so long and proceed so hesitantly?

The Young Henrietta, by Verelst.

Henrietta (St. John) Lady Luxborough. English School.

I

*Henry, 1st Viscount St. John in coronation robes
(Henrietta's father), artist unknown.*

*Angelica Magdalena, 1st Viscountess St. John in coronation robes
(Henrietta's mother), artist unknown.*

Henry, 1st Viscount Bolingbroke as a young man. Henrietta's half brother, by Smart.

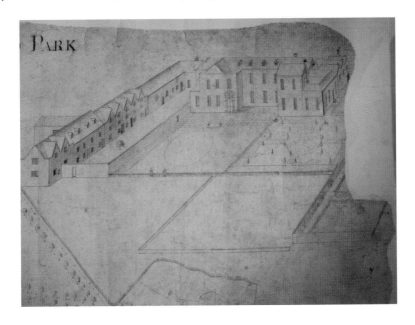

Detail of Map c.1700, showing the West Front of Lydiard House.

III

Robert Knight as a young man, artist unknown.

Robert Knight, Henrietta's husband (Lord Luxborough and Earl Catherlough),
by Thomas Hudson.

The Hon. Henrietta Knight, Henrietta's daughter. Attributed to Joseph Highmore.

The Hon. Henry Knight, Henrietta's son. Attributed to Joseph Highmore.

Frances Thynne, Lady Hertford, later Duchess of Somerset.
Attributed to Thomas Hudson.

Elizabeth Rowe. Artist unknown.

VI

A view of Battersea c.1750. From an engraving for the Royal Magazine.

Bolingbroke House (Battersea Manor). From an original woodcut. Date unknown.

The Cedar Room, Battersea Manor. From a photograph c.1911.

Ceiling of Cedar Room, illustrating delicate strapwork plaster.
From a photograph c.1911.

That they would have spent time together in France, either at La Planchette with Robert Knight senior or with Bolingbroke at La Source is likely, for the young Robert frequently visited his father in the early seventeen twenties. He also spent time at Bolingbroke's La Source from where, in letters home, the latter extolled the many virtues of his young friend, finding him to be "a man of letters, a man of sense and a man of proberty" [5], the most important attribute being left until last.

So it was that when Henrietta again visited her brother in France in the summer of 1725, the ground had been carefully prepared. Against the backdrop of a chorus of approval from her brother and sister-in-law, she would have been propelled forward and love match or not, it is likely that she would have fallen in love with the idea of marriage if not with the man, himself. All this is surmise but what follows is not. By this time the St Johns wanted to see Henrietta settled. Family finances were not as robust as they once had been and the interest upon £10,000 which Lord St John was to leave his daughter in his will, when compared, for example with the £5,000 that Lady Vane dispensed upon a piece of garden frippery, assumes a disproportionate modesty. Such an alliance was also attractive to the Knight family. Of yeoman stock, their son's marriage into the aristocracy would set the seal upon their social aspirations.

So were all the pieces of the jigsaw set in place. But there must have been uncertainties because it still took a further two years before the couple finally married and surely these are likely to have originated with Henrietta?

Hesitation or not, when the time came the marriage settlement is of interest. This required that Lord St John contribute £6,000 down with a promise that upon his death there would be a realizable bond of an additional £2,000. Mr Knight, senior's, contribution was considerably more. He settled £34,000 upon the couple which provided a total of £40,000 to be invested in land. Out of this, £12,000 was to be set aside for Henrietta to provide her with an income of some £500 per annum. It would seem that this was an agreement which favoured the St John family and a reasonable conclusion must be that this union, whether a love match or not, had much to do with expediency.

Eventually, in the St John tradition, the couple married at St Mary's little Church at Battersea on 20 June 1727. They were married by special licence by the Reverend Osbourne and although there is no mention of a honeymoon, were soon to set up house in London's Grosvenor Street prior to making a bid for William Chetwynd's house in Dover Street. It was a bid to be brokered by Bolingbroke and one that was doomed to fail when he advised the young couple that the asking price was exorbitant and persuaded them "by no means" to offer more than "the great price" to which they were already committed. Negotiations broke down and the Knights were obliged to remain in Grosvenor Street, a small disappointment, perhaps, but one which within the early context of this marriage, may be seen as symptomatic of what was to follow. But at first all would appear to have been well and Bolingbroke was moved in October of that same year to thank the young couple "for all the experience of kindness and friendship which I have received" [6], at their home.

But much can happen in a month. By November the peace of Grosvenor Street was about to be shattered for Mr Knight, senior, was demanding his dues. Still unable to return to Britain, still isolated at La Planchette, his splendid estate outside Paris that he had bought with doubtful money, he now wished his daughter-in-law to take over the management of his household. This was because his second wife was ill, and having, as he saw it, contributed so richly to the couple's future, his request was a command rather than a favour.

That Henrietta did not wish to uproot herself is clear. As always when under stress she was ill with one of her incipient "feavours", and Bolingbroke's encouraging letter to his sister at this time could do little more than exhort her to make the best of things. "You are surely very much in the right to comply with Mr Knight's desire" [7] he writes and maintains that her deteriorating health will benefit from a change of air.

From now on, Henrietta's marriage was to become increasingly peripatetic as she trundled miserably between London and Paris. Her first visit after the marriage was in December 1727, when upon arrival she was ill enough to take to her bed. By February she was back in London and pregnant with her first child, Henry; and this was when rumours apparently fuelled by Thomas Coke, later Lord Lovell, began to circulate. It was suggested that visits to her doctor, the respected Dr Peters, were for reasons other than medical advice, and as the weeks wore on, like Chinese Whispers, the claims became ever more bizarre. It was not long before Peters and Henrietta were alleged to have been surprised in bed together, a claim which must have reached her husband's ear and one to which, surprisingly, he made no public response. One wonders why? Instead it was left to Bolingbroke to defend his sister's honour from the pen of Thomas Coke, his one time whoring companion. To whom, years ago in October 1704, he had written: "As to whores, dear friend I am... unable to help thee" although he has:

> heard of a certain housemaid that is very handsome, if she can be got ready for your arrival, she shall serve as your first meal[8].

Perhaps it is worth pausing for a moment to consider this Lord Lovell who was to become the Member of Parliament for Derbyshire and who, as did Bolingbroke, lived by the dual standards of the day. It was a way of life which did not prevent them from falling out, however, and Henrietta's brother responded robustly in words which hint of his sister's distress. "As to the scandalous story which has given you so much trouble... you ought to despise both it... and the whisperers of it". Lovell, he asserts: "is a stranger to delicacy and decency"[9].

A further problem for this marriage was created by the long periods of separation to which the couple were subject. Frequently while Henrietta was at La Planchette, her husband was absent in London where his work as a Member of Parliament was carried out; and if his future conduct, to be considered later, is anything to go by, it is unlikely that during these periods he would have foregone the pleasures of female company.

Neither should we forget the surprise with which Henrietta's choice of a husband had been viewed by her friends. Writing to Lady Hertford after the wedding, Mrs Rowe was to posit her belief that: "nothing but an Adonis would have pleased Mrs Knight's temper", even though she supposed that Henrietta's "gentle disposition and good sense would enable her to make the best of things" [10]. From someone who knew her so well, a comment far from encouraging. Later, Horace Walpole's malicious description of Knight, "a little wizen husband", although not necessarily accurate, would seem to make the same point – that Mrs Knight could and, indeed should have done better for herself.

During the seven short years of her married life, Henrietta was obliged to divide her time between Paris and London – a fact which meant that neither venue felt like home. It was a marriage on the move and one which affected her health and emotional well being. At La Planchette, her father-in-law entertained extravagantly and Mrs Knight, in her capacity as hostess, was caught up and propelled along by the elder Knight's repeated and energetic attempts to "buy" his way back into respectability. English visitors of any perceived influence were welcome and so out of hand did things become, that even Bolingbroke was moved to write disapprovingly to Henrietta concerning her father-in-law's self-indulgent life style. He wishes that the company with whom she "must do the honours (was) better chosen" and in response to her complaints, is sympathetic to a state of affairs which means that she has "many honours to do which will oftener tire than delight" [11].

It is only in her long letters home that Henrietta can reveal her true dislike of the environs of La Planchette which appear contrived and artificial; of a trip to the Paris Opera which only serves to remind her of the 'better' ways of the London theatre. She writes of a grand hunting party on a neighbouring estate as "distasteful" and "boring" and the impression created is of a most unhappy young woman. But she does enjoy the occasional country walk – alone – with a copy of *Il Pastor Fido* in her pocket, a reminder of carefree days with Frances Hertford and Elizabeth Rowe at Marlborough Castle.

To Frances, Henrietta describes the tenor of life at La Planchette. It is sterile; "a hurrying life" which allows no time for contemplation – one in which "the pleasures of the mind are denied". A life in which "eating and play" with those she has little in common, takes up her time. Her days are long and arduous. She rises at nine and is seldom permitted to retire before two in the morning. Her daily programme is not of her own choosing. It is "just what the family pleases"; usually the wining and dining of "a multitude of English young men" [12], including the Duke of Richmond or Lord Dursley or any aristocrat who can be tempted to visit. Later, her duties include the organization of card tables – the offering of drinks and light refreshments.

During these hectic times two children were born to Henrietta and her husband: a son, Henry on 28 December 1728, and a daughter, Henrietta, on 21 November 1729. But Mrs Knight, although an excellent mother, was not permitted to spend much time with them – just two hours a day if she were lucky: and frequently they were not with her at all as it suited her husband and father-in-law to have them left behind with the Hertfords in England. Family life, such as it was, took second place to the demands and whims of an increasingly cantankerous Mr Knight, senior.

Even as late as 1734, Henrietta's peripatetic domestic life showed little sign of slowing down. When in England, the Knights returned to their house in Grosvenor Street which served as a headquarters from which to make visits to the Hertfords at Marlborough or St Leonards; the St John houses at Battersea or Lydiard Tregoze. And increasingly it was once again with Frances that Henrietta felt most at home.

It was possibly in 1734, on one of her frequent visits to Marlborough Castle that Henrietta first met Mr Dalton, the young Oxford educated clergyman employed by the Hertfords as tutor to their son and heir, Lord Beauchamp. Dalton was younger than Henrietta, many of the young men with whom she became friendly later in life, were. He was good looking, well read and good fun. She was attractive, vivacious and always eager to learn. They shared similar interests – enjoyed literature and the reading and writing of poetry. Dalton was everything that Robert Knight was not. He was sensitive and cultured and his attractive appearance enhanced his appeal. An appeal which, incidentally, was also felt by Elizabeth Rowe and Frances Hertford.

So it was not long before the young clergyman was invited to join in the deliberations of these three rhyming letter writers, committed to the spinning of "fun" verses which tell of inconsequential things; are sentimental, romantic, expansive and innocent enough for Lady Hertford to record in her commonplace-book, for posterity. Now the young women were to pen verses to Dalton as well as to each other, and he was quick to respond in kind with compliments and all manner of amusing nonsense.

It was in April 1734, at a time when Henrietta was unwell and unable to join their party, that Dalton sent Mrs Knight his verses "Upon Leaving London for St Leonard's Hall". The last four lines are worth pondering a moment, for they could be construed as flirtatious:

> *One charm I own remains behind,*
> *Till Marion with each Muse come's down*
> *With Cupid Monarch of mankind,*
> *I pity then the empty town* [13].

Here, the near positioning of "Marion" with "Cupid" could be significant – but not necessarily, especially as Marion's prompt response which catches the mood of the "game":

> *No sooner was Adonis fled*
> *To breath Parnassian air*
> *But I with sorrow dropp'd my head*
> *And tore my platted hair* [14].

is amusing mock tragedy – but nothing more.

So the quartet entertained themselves, innocently enough. However, a final tribute in the series from Dalton to Henrietta is possibly of more significance. This is because the verses might indicate that "the game" is now being played out in reality. The first and last stanzas will suffice to demonstrate. The poem begins, moderately enough.

Yes, Lovely Marion, I submit
I bow to beauty and to wit
To you I bow, to whom belong
The charms of beauty and of song.

The tone is light hearted, the compliments playful, and it is not until the final stanza that a new dimension is, possibly, introduced.

Give me the Friendship of my Fair,
Give me that something still more Dear –
In Love's light Plumes be others drest
I ask no more – that to be blest [15].

What, one wonders, is "that something" more dear than friendship? Love, of course. On the other hand, "Love's light Plumes" appear to be for others – and the enigmatic last line can be interpreted in different ways.

Is there evidence here for a dazzled and lovesick John Dalton? Some might believe so. But thus far at least, there is surely nothing other than witty and playful reciprocity from Henrietta, committed only to a warm friendship.

Even so, it was not to be long before the situation accelerated and Mrs Knight's life irrevocably changed. What happened; how and why, provides material for the next chapter.

Chapter 5

SCANDAL

In October of 1734, Henrietta's father-in-law sent her at home in Grosvenor Street in London a friendly message:

> *...when you think of any commission for me at Paris, I hope you won't need to be assured that your commands will always be acceptable to me* [1].

Nearly a decade later, as his reply to an invitation from Henrietta to visit her at Barrells, in June 1743 makes clear, the climate has changed. Upon his return to England, his tone is now as different as the nightingale's song from a raven's croak:

> *I have received your letter but your conduct towards my son has been such that it does not admit of any correspondence between us* [2].

What has happened?

The search for an answer, definitive or not, points to the story of Henrietta's "disgrace" and subsequent exile to Barrells. It is a story which poses as many questions as answers; and picking one's way through a fog of lies, half-truths and innuendo, is far from easy. So perhaps it is sensible to begin with what *is* known. That Mrs Knight was accused of an affair with John Dalton, tutor to the Hertford's son, Lord Beauchamp, is fact. That it was rumoured she had become pregnant by him, is also fact. But rumour may, or may not, be based upon truth, and can sometimes serve to muddy clear waters.

One of the leading figures in this "drama", was Henrietta's influential father-in-law, Robert Knight, senior. A contemporary description of him is hardly flattering. He was:

A man of some parts, of an address far above his birth or former manner of life (which I think had been that of a tradesman), very insinuating... yet close and dextrous in management of the trusts he undertook [3].

That he was "close and dextrous" in the management of his own affairs and those of his family, is certainly true. That at the time of Henrietta's marriage, he was living at "an address far above his birth or former manner of life", is also true. As was the orgy of speculation in which as cashier of the ill-fated South Sea Company, he had been involved. A situation which had led to unsustainable share prices and in turn, financial ruin for many. The corrosive effects of these dubious proceedings had led to the bursting of The South Sea Bubble, as it came to be called, and reached into the highest ranks of government office – even the Court itself. Such a man who, with the help of influential friends, had managed to evade British justice and bribe his way home from France, was not one to be trifled with. More importantly, neither was his son, Henrietta's husband, over whom he exerted influence and who had inherited the same implacability which was to make any attempt at reconciliation impossible.

In the previous chapter, we left Henrietta, Lady Hertford, Elizabeth Rowe and John Dalton engaged in some light-hearted versification. However, in the winter of 1734–1735, when Mrs Knight's return to England was celebrated by an especially long stay at Marlborough Castle with her friends, Lord and Lady Hertford, things took a more ominous turn. Over the previous months, Henrietta's letters to Frances had been fuelled with anticipatory excitement at the thought of again being part of that harmonious household; not only of seeing Frances and her husband but their daughter, Lady Betty, their son and heir Lord Beauchamp, and of course his tutor, John Dalton, with whom there had been much enjoyable fun. So upon her arrival, it is not surprising that she was quick to take up again the reins of friendship.

It was not to be long before the old times returned and the women resumed their amusing verse letters, a game in which, as before, John Dalton was invited to join. Soon, little notes and poems were passing frequently between Dalton and Henrietta; scribbled messages which at first were a continuation of conversations enjoyed earlier in the day, but which as the weeks passed, became more intimate – more private and personal; for Dalton was receptive and it is likely that Henrietta penned those thoughts which she could not communicate to her husband. Ideas which for too long had been denied expression amid the card playing, the hunting parties and the incessant comings and goings of La Planchette.

How delightful it was – how reassuring to live again among like-minded people. Those who read, had thoughts and feelings akin to her own and who with every expression of good will, gave the lie to that now far away and alien life she had been obliged to endure in France.

Delightful, yes! But it was not to last... for before long and almost one feels, on cue, a scribbled little piece by Henrietta to the young tutor was discovered by her husband:

> *As soon as you were gone I employed myself (as it must ever be in something that suggests you) in reading over your letters which I have resolved to burn, but could not bring my heart or hand to execute...*

And later on in the same letter:

> *I can't help remembering the time when one hour or two brought me some publick or private letter of your passionate, tender sentiments wrote in your own hand* [4].

The note, allowed in Bolingbroke's words, "to lye loose around", did not at the time strike Mrs Knight as especially important. With hindsight she was to see things differently; then it would seem to have been foolish and fanciful – the fruits of an over-ripe friendship – and nothing more. But was that all?

When confronted by a furious Robert Knight, Henrietta's defence never wavered. The lines, she maintained, were not of her own composition, but copies of translations of romantic "nonsense" which she had, at any rate, intended to burn. In her own words:

> *I have read this over which in my first surprise I did not do and I am now sure more than ever, that I never wrote it as the dictates of my own heart; and... I was imprudent as to translate and copy out a large Bundle of such foolish letters 13 of which I burn'd last week to make room for things I was placing...* [5].

A careful reading of the full "incriminating" letter might indicate that what she says is in part true, for the style of the two extracts above, taken from the beginning and the end of her note is not consistent. Words in the opening sentence, for example, are formal: "employed", "resolved" and "execute" do not sound at all like the spontaneous outpourings of the warm-hearted Henrietta. The impression created is quite different from that of the later passage in which the adjectives "passionate", "tender" and the phrase, "wrote in your own hand", have a spontaneity and warmth which is more representative of the person she was.

In the same letter to Dalton, Henrietta quotes a passage from one of **his** to her:

> *I love you still more and must ever do so unless you pour into my wounded soul the clear balm of your compassion and teach me by gentle means to overcome it* [6].

There would seem to be little doubt here. Dalton had been infatuated with Henrietta – a young woman whom he would have perceived as sophisticated and beautiful; who, for all her feminine charm, could think and discuss ideas with the verve of a man. But now his ardour was cooling – or maybe he had come to realize how unsustainable his situation was. One in which Mrs Knight had acted as requested – had taught him "by gentle means to overcome it". Only too successfully, it would seem, because his "passion is conquered" and she is now left wishing that the same "remedy" might cure her as well.

But in the end, perhaps it does not matter how much of her letter was Henrietta's own – except to show that she was not a liar. For there can be no doubt that the two were close; that each realized the "goings on", whatever they were, must stop. Mrs Knight's use of "the means to conquer it", and "time alone can work the cure", is as indicative of her understanding of the situation as Dalton's apparent coldness is of his.

Much has been made of Henrietta's penultimate line that "virtue has not prevailed"; mistakenly, for this must surely refer to her feelings and not to any resultant action. That she perceives her feelings to be wrong is not in question but there is little hard evidence to suggest that there was any resultant adultery. In spite of the gossip, the scandal-mongers and the whisperers, it is unlikely that the two were lovers, although rumours of an illegitimate child, born at Barrells where Henrietta lived in exile, has been fuelled by Horace Walpole's, "They rhymed together until they chimed"; a wittily malicious description of their interest in poetry. An early edition of the *Dictionary of National Biography* carries the same story, one that is eliminated from later editions.

And the rumours do not fit with fact. In the autumn of 1735, when she was living in exile at Barrells, we find Henrietta requesting and being refused permission to visit her favourite Aunt Cholmondeley who was seriously ill. Neither a heavily pregnant Mrs Knight, nor one who had recently given birth, would have contemplated such an arduous journey in an unsprung coach. Then there is the question of Dalton, himself, a young man who remained happily in the employ of the Hertfords for many years and to whose good auspices he owed the steady advancement of his career. The Hertfords were admirable people and it is inconceivable that they would not have dispensed with his services, let alone furthered his prospects, if they had believed him to be the father of an illegitimate child – especially if the mother were one of their dearest friends.

Even so, the St Johns judged Henrietta and found her guilty. They closed ranks, held conferences and wrote letters that abound with double-speak and innuendo. They sided with the aggrieved husband and even applauded the part that he was to play in the shaping of Mrs Knight's future. Bolingbroke writes enigmatically to Henrietta about "the unhappy affair", urging "moderation". But that he thinks her guilty is implicit in what he has to say to the angry husband: "...this eclat being made there is no more to be said" [7]. Another of Mrs Knight's brothers, the duplicitous Jack St John is more explicit. "If I had been her husband", he writes to Robert Knight, "My God, I would have dated my Ease and Happiness from the hour she gave me a justifiable cause to part with her..." [8]. A sentiment which is likely to have approximated with Mr Knight's own view; a man who could have seized upon his wife's foolishness to be rid of her as her bright intellect had served to widen the intellectual chasm that divided them.

But in any case, writing to his sister a week later and signing himself "...your affectionate Brother and true Friend", St John, shows a different face. So, round and round the letters run whilst in the meantime, the distraught Henrietta appeals again and again to her husband. As early as October 1734 when the storm had first broken, is her first attempt:

> *My dearest Life for God's sake consider what effect our parting will have and try to bring yourself to be under the same roof as me...* [9].

She insists that what was once a "silly but Platonick passion", is now at an end and pleads "the most terrible affliction" that she is suffering. It met with no response and neither was her family prepared to mediate. Early in 1736, and after numerous abortive attempts she tries again. Like a prisoner pleading for life, the words resonate with an abject humility:

> *For God's sake let me see you and ask your pardon on my knees... but yet I swear the passion was Platonick and is no more...* [10].

They provide food for thought. As has been seen, the "scandal" first surfaced in the autumn of 1734: and now by October 1736, after a period of two years Henrietta is still pleading her cause. Would she (one must ask) have continued to solicit her husband in this vein if she were now the mother of an illegitimate child?

To return to the facts – there is little doubt that Robert Knight had convinced himself of Henrietta's "transgressions"; that he had come to lose any feelings for her that he once may have had. However, extracts from his commonplace-book support the view that he did once love her. In it he writes of "a sacred cherished lady (Henrietta?)... a name still to be uttered with a sigh" – but whose "last ungraceful scene has quite effaced all sense and memory of your former worth". He writes of envy, "the meagre slave of sore revenge" and of anger. He quotes from scripture, "Let not the sun go down upon your wrath" [11] – but, in his wife's case, was unwilling to translate this into action, remaining adamant that they must never meet again.

His response was to offer her a choice. She could remain in his house, locked away upstairs on a top floor (the attic?) without pen or paper or books to entertain herself. It was a choice which meant that she would be denied access to the outside world or even to the garden – for the two must never meet again and Robert Knight did not wish to be reminded of her existence. Alternatively, she could choose exile in his tumbledown farmhouse, Barrells Green, at Ullenhall, a hamlet near Henley-in-Arden, in Warwickshire. Both choices were to mean that she would forfeit all visits to London, to Marlborough Castle or anywhere that she was likely to feel at home [12]. Either locked away or deposited in the middle of nowhere, as it would have seemed then, she was to be deprived of her children and air-brushed out of society as if she had never existed.

It is not surprising that at first Henrietta was to find, "the alternatives given me are so severe that it is difficult to choose" [13]. Indeed it was; for to balance the harshness of, "the being confined to one Floor – being deprived of so small a comfort as that of Ink and Paper" [14], with the misery of isolation in the middle of the country where she had no friends and knew nobody, was near to impossible.

At first, and counter to family advice, Henrietta was inclined to choose exile. "Liberty is so sweet that it is more natural for me to choose... a remote cottage Free, than to remain at home a prisoner..." [15]. However, the advice of her family finally prevailed and she eventually agreed to remain locked upstairs at home, with the proviso that should her health fail, she might still have recourse to banishment in the country.

Of course, it was not long before she did become ill. She put on weight through lack of exercise and was consequently and not very kindly referred to by her sister-in-law, Marie Claire, as "our fat Fan Fan", a family nick name. Henrietta became lethargic and her mental health suffered. Things soon so deteriorated that her roué of a father, Lord St John, relented. He changed sides, deciding that the country option – any option – would be preferable to the present and as we might see it, medieval, state of affairs.

So, Mrs Knight was sent to Barrells. But not before, in her heart-broken way, she had continued to plead her cause, protesting against her husband's "unjust suspicions".

But Knight was always to be content with the way things were. Freedom beckoned – and the opportunity presented to him by his wife was to be taken. Towards the end of their marriage there had been problems. His wife on occasion had not been so submissive as he would have liked. She had a mind of her own and an intellect to match and there had been – differences. Problems that came with an intelligent and vivacious wife were now at an end and he looked to the future. And one thing is clear; nothing illustrates the power of the eighteenth century husband more than this sorry episode in the life of Henrietta Knight; obliged as she was, to re-invent herself in a new life which, as later chapters show, she lived with exemplary courage. The road was to be arduous, as without her children and without a husband, without the security of familiar faces and places, she set out to take on the future – quite alone.

Chapter 6

EXILE

The house was in bad repair. When Henrietta arrived: "There were not half the windows up, no doors to the house, and the roof uncovered" [1]. But it did have, from the family's point of view, two great advantages. It was away from London still busy with the buzz of "scandal", and it was conveniently in the country where an errant wife could be hidden away.

The property, known as Barrells, Barrells Green or Barrells Hall, derived its name from the first owner of the land in 1327. It was acquired by an earlier Robert Knight in 1554 and nearly a century later, in 1662, was described in an inventory of "the goods and chattels" of Nicholas Knight as an ordinary timber framed farm house. When Henrietta's husband bought the property in 1730, it had belonged in the family for nearly two hundred years and was at present owned by a cousin of his, Raleigh Knight, who would seem to have been experiencing financial problems: a fact which no doubt reflected upon the price at which it was purchased.

The farmhouse was situated in Ullenhall, or Ullenbeorge, another of the names by which this hamlet in a quiet corner of Warwickshire, was originally known. On the borders of what is now the thriving market town of Henley-in-Arden and some eleven miles from Stratford-upon-Avon, the village was also fifteen miles from Birmingham – then a little town "embowered with trees"; with bowling greens and tea gardens to amuse its mere fifteen hundred souls.

As far as Henrietta was concerned, and once she had begun to come to terms with her situation, the property did have advantages. On her land were a number of tenant farmers with whom she was obliged to have some contact, and views from the house across a gently undulating landscape were some of the best in the country. Then there was the proximity of Lord Somervile's Edstone Estate where she was to become a frequent visitor and, in summertime, the lure of William Shenstone's Leasowes at Halesowen. Yes... there were possibilities here – but that was in the future.

Precisely when Mrs Knight was despatched to Barrells is not known. But her brother Bolingbroke's response to one of her early letters: "I am rejoiced to hear that your books and your gardens can do so well in your solitude"[2], suggests that by as early as March 1736, some order was already emerging from the chaos. It also points the way that Henrietta was to take with her gardening and literary activities as centre stage.

With her, Mrs Knight had been permitted to take a number of servants, a concession wrung from her husband who insisted that their number be minimal. She was allowed to take her lady's maid – an imperative, for at the time her health was poor and due to "that damp ditch she's been thrown into"[3], remained so for some time. Altogether, one is left with an impression of deprivation: of cold, draught and poverty which defies credulity. That she was to survive, let alone embark upon a loving and painful restoration of the house, was a minor miracle – one to be detailed later on – and that she had the will to move forward and make new friends, no less so.

Even so, and surprisingly, it does not seem to have been overlong before she accomplished just that. It was the local clergy who first extended the hand of friendship; men who were, on the whole, a close knit and kindly group. Who were the product of an excellent grounding in the Classics and frequently chose to enliven their none too burdensome lives with the writing of poetry, pastoral and pretty. Men who would accept with alacrity invitations to dine at the tables of their wealthy neighbours – who enjoyed walks around country estates, offering guidance upon the placing of a memorial urn, or the appropriate wording for an inscription. In Henrietta's letters, these are her friends who appear and re-appear like familiar characters in a play. Men for whom, in some instances, the taking of holy orders had opened a door into a world of civilized living; who as Mrs Knight's new intimates, were to involve her in stepping daintily down the social ladder, yet not a rung so far or so obvious as to make her regret the opulent life-style she had left.

One of the most important of their number was Richard Jago (senior), Rector of Beaudesert in Henley-in-Arden from 1709 until his death in 1740 at the age of sixty-one. At the time Henrietta arrived upon the scene, he was a well-known and established parish priest and it was to be at his rectory that she was first to meet his son, also Richard and also a clergyman. This Richard Jago was in turn to introduce Mrs Knight to his close friend, the poet, William Shenstone, with whom he had been a pupil at Solihull School which still boasts a House named after him. Both young men were soon to become loyal members of Henrietta's Coterie, a group of local writers who were later entertained at Barrells and about whom there is more discussion in the following chapter.

It was also by means of Richard Jago (senior) that Mrs Knight was to meet Parson Allen, the incumbent of Spernal, a parish which lies between Coughton and Studley. Parson Allen was frequently to be seen at Barrells. A great talker, he seems to have had little concern for the clock and with his "stories" would frequently keep Mrs Knight from her bed until the small hours. This was the gentleman whose literary efforts were so to annoy Shenstone. One who although "he does not pretend to be a poet", was confident enough to "correct" a poetical offering to Henrietta from a fellow parson, a Mr Perks of Coughton. The story is worth telling. Mr Perks had apparently heard of the beauties of Barrells and determined, although he had never seen the place, to write about them. As Henrietta was to inform Shenstone:

> *I never saw (him) but twice; and he had never seen Barrells when he wrote it, but came to see it, in order to make his Dedication in praise of it* [4].

It was an omission which does not seem to have deterred the indefatigable parson:

Here ev'ry flow'r that decks th'enamelled meade
Or thro' the grove its vernal beauty spreads,
In lively tints so natural so true
A piece more perfect Titian never drew –

Whose work also includes an unsuitable description of the sea which does not chime readily with the realities of an inland country garden!

See heaps of shells, old Ocean's glassy store
Have left their briny cells and weep no more
Beneath the rolling waves no long sleep,
Swept from the rocks and caverns of the deep:... [5].

Unknown to Mr Perks, there is irony here; for one of the few things that Henrietta was to regret about her garden at Barrells was its dearth of water: no streams, pools or fishponds to create contrasting waterscapes such as there were in abundance at her friend William Shenstone's Leasowes. And ridiculous though the poem is, within a social context it is not without interest. In an age of patronage and in his limited way, Mr Perks would have been aspiring to please a possible patron and a fine lady of quality. So it was that complete with its Dedication, Henrietta enclosed a copy of the manuscript in a letter to her friend, Shenstone, who received it with amusement and not a little irritation at the sight of Allen's name affixed to the front which read:

A DEDICATION OF A PASTORAL
ELEGY HUMBLY IMITATED

(Mr Perk's Dedication to Lady Luxborough,
corrected by Parson Allen) [6].

43

For Shenstone, himself, had suffered similar problems with Parson Allen. It concerned the writing of an inscription – an art-form at which the poet excelled and one in which he did not seek or expect to be offered unwelcome advice. But it would seem that Allen had a thick skin; he persisted and Shenstone in a huff suggested that if he thought that he could do better with his meddling, then he had better do it!

Another member of this group was Parson Hall, "an intimate acquaintance and schoolfellow" of Shenstone. Probably Henrietta was introduced to him by Shenstone although he, too, would have known Jago so it might have been the latter. Thomas Hall was to become a great favourite of Henrietta and the more intimate members of her "Coterie". This "little round oily man of God"[7] whose Assize Sermon caused wry amusement when passed around the group, its contents to be described, deliciously and enigmatically by Shenstone as applying "many scripture phrases very spirituously"[8]. It is a comment with more than a hint of what he must have sounded like from the pulpit.

Other country parsons with whom Mrs Knight became friendly included John (Jacky) Reynolds, Chaplain to Lord Somervile; the Reverend John Perry, a minor poet whose "Malvern Spa" was to be included in Volume V of Robert Dodsley's *Miscellanies,* a Collection of verse which in Henrietta's day was very popular. But the most important of all these men was the Reverend William Holyoake, Rector of Oldberrow which at one time fell within the confines of the Barrells' Estate. Both parson and doctor, this was the man who became Henrietta's Chaplain and who ministered to both her spiritual and medical needs. He and his motherly wife, a lady in many ways akin to Shenstone's housekeeper, Mrs Arnold, became very close to Mrs Knight, providing support, comfort and security throughout her life at Barrells. It was Holyoake who was to notify Shenstone of her Ladyship's death; he it was and his wife who were constantly at her bedside throughout her final illness. He it is who figures most prominently throughout Henrietta's letters.

On stage and off, these men are representative of the country parsons who lived in the environs of Barrells in the mid seventeen hundreds. They belonged to a community which provided an invaluable link between peasant and gentry – tradesman and aristocrat. They are the men, who, together with their families, were to play a vital role in Henrietta's rehabilitation and help to make for her a brighter future than would otherwise have been imaginable.

Chapter 7

THE COTERIE

During her time at Barrells. Henrietta was to gather around her a group of local writers who were to become known as "The Warwickshire Coterie", deriving their name from the county where most of them lived. The best known of the group and the friend with whom she became most intimate was the poet, William Shenstone, but others who were frequent visitors included William Somervile, a local squire, Richard Jago, junior, and Richard Graves. Another member, Anthony Whistler, did not live locally but was invited as a friend of Shenstone's when he was staying with the poet at the Leasowes in Halesowen.

William Somervile was the oldest and earliest member of the "Coterie". Born in 1675, he was a popular "huntin and shootin" squire who had also time to write some not inconsiderable verse. His poem, *The Chase*, published in 1735, was to crown his literary career and became a talking point in literary circles. The poem which runs into four volumes, is of interest – not for the picture it paints of the death of a young hart from exhaustion, her "reeking entrails and yet quivering heart" thrown to the hounds as a reward "for all their toil"; but as the record of a way of life. Somervile hunted every day and what the work has to say, for example, concerning the care and kennelling of fox-hounds, the duties of chief huntsman and so on, is invaluable.

Somervile and the younger Richard Jago, Shenstone's school friend, were frequent visitors at Barrells in the later seventeen thirties, so it was only a matter of time before the poet was to appear on the scene. We know that he was introduced to Henrietta by Jago because she tells us so in a letter to that same young man in November 1739:

To you, Sir, I owe the pleasure of having enjoyed that gentleman's conversation a few moments; to you I owe the advantage of being represented to him in the most flattering light [1].

By this time Shenstone has already begun to send Mrs Knight some of his verses and her delight in what she has read is clear in her entreaty that Jago will make known to his friend:

"the sincerity of my heart in the approbation it gives to his works" [2].

It was encouragement of the sort that Shenstone relished and he responded with more verses and soon – presumably – letters.

Jago and Shenstone had been pupils at Solihull School together where they found that they had much in common. Both were keen classical scholars – had a love of Virgil and of English Literature, too. By their early teens, both were reading Virgil and Shakespeare for pleasure. In his long auto-biographical poem *Edgehill*, Jago tells of their holidays when the two boys would ramble along the banks of the Avon, acutely aware that they were treading in the bard's footsteps:

...range in solitary shades
and scoop rude grottoes in the shelving banks – [3],

an image of children making mud-pies hallowed by the bard's memory.

In middle age, Shenstone was to recall those early days of friendship with Henrietta Knight as she then was. He writes of a balmy summer's evening in 1739, when he first shared a bench seat with Somervile under the canopy of Barrells' famous "double oak". Jago would have been there, too, and surely the talk would have turned to poetry. Perhaps Somervile's affectionate description of his old hunting dog from Canto 1 of *The Chase*:

...Now grown stiff with age
and many a painful chase, the wise old hound
Regardless of the frolic pack, attends
His master's side, or slumbers at his ease
Beneath the bending shade, there many a ring
'Runs o'er in dreams [4].

Or they might have listened to Shenstone recite his *When Fair Ophelia Treads the Green*, a "song" that he had hopes "to translate into music":

When bright Ophelia treads the green
In all the pride of dress and mien
Averse to freedom, mirth and play
The lofty rival of my day;
Methinks to my enchanted eye,
The lilies droop, the roses die [5].

Then it might have been Jago's turn to recite his poem, *Peto's Ghost*, which tells of an apparition which appeared to him, late one night, when on his way home from a meeting in Warwick:

...thro the dark and lonesome shade
Shone forth a sudden light [6]:

It is a piece which reflects Jago's interest in the supernatural. He was of Cornish descent and his family had occult powers – or so it was believed. His great great grandfather, also a clergyman, had earned himself a considerable reputation as a ghost layer. In one of his more notable cases, he had "horse whipped" the apparition of a Jew who, in order to wreak revenge, had hanged himself outside his enemy's house so that every night he might return to haunt him!

Whilst a well loved priest in the Warwickshire parish of Harbury, Shenstone's Jago was also to experience ghostly problems. His parishioners were to be frightened by a ghost in the graveyard and in response to their request for aid, he preached a sermon on the following Sunday with its theme of "Extraordinary Warnings". What help this was – if any – is not recorded. But Jago had the contents printed, anyway, and offered them to anyone who showed an interest.

Shenstone does not record the presence, on this occasion, of the fourth and fifth members of the Coterie, Richard Graves and Anthony Whistler. The three had met while up at Oxford and the former was to become a successful novelist and the poet's first biographer. His *Recollections of Some Particulars in the Life of the Late William Shenstone Esquire",* sets out to vindicate the poet's reputation which had suffered at the hands of Dr Johnson in his *Lives of the Poets.* In it he tells of an invitation to breakfast with Shenstone at his rooms, which was how their life-long friendship started.

Destined for an academic career which he was obliged to forego, Graves also was ordained. In spite of opposition from his family – his father was Lord of the Manor at Mickleton in Gloucestershire – he married his charming Lucy, a yeoman's daughter and embarked upon what was to turn out to be a very happy marriage. He had met the girl whilst staying as a young priest with her family near Oxford and although she became pregnant by him, the story is not as unfortunate as it might sound. Graves was a decent man at heart and his decision to marry the girl turned out to have been the right one.

After the birth of their first child, Lucy was sent to London, to a finishing school, to be taught the manners of a "lady" – proper to her future role as the wife of a country clergyman. The separation, although brief, caused them both distress and in his charming little poem *The Parting*, Graves describes how it must have felt:

> *But oh! The fated hour has come*
> *That forced me from my dear;*
> *My Lucy that through grief was dumb*
> *Or spake but by a tear.*

Nay life itself is tasteless grown
From Lucy whist I stray
Sick of the world I muse alone
And sigh the live long day [7].

It is a poem which was to "do the rounds" of the Coterie who, on the whole, were supportive of his situation. But Henrietta's reaction expresses a perplexity and displays a logic which was to cause Shenstone some discomfort. "Why" she was to ask, since Graves (because of what he had done) "May be supposed to despise the opinion of the world", and, "since he married so much beneath himself and what the world would recommend", does he then proceed to obtain for his wife an education to "please that world which he seems to despise?" [8]

Answering this, Shenstone, ever a loyal friend to both, must have felt like a tight rope walker over Niagara Falls as he struggled to support the action of Graves, on the one hand, without giving offence to a lady of quality on the other. His response makes for interesting reading.

Your Ladyship's sentiment is very ingenious; but we will suppose he prefers his
Lucy to the good opinion of the wise world, yet he doesn't so entirely despise that
opinion as not to wish to compromise matters [9].

Surely a reply that would not disgrace the wiliest of politicians! One in which the poet, with consummate skill, makes his own brand of compromise.

But to return to 1739 and that summer evening at Barrells where Henrietta was fulfilling a role for which she had been schooled all those years ago at Marlborough Castle with her literary friends. How she must have cherished her newly resurrected self-esteem; enjoyed the conversation of literary men, reminiscent of the times she had spent with her brother Bolingbroke and his guests – Alexander Pope and "Johney" Gay at his "farm" at Dawley. (See Chapter 11).

Henrietta with her Latin eyes and lustrous dark hair who was to exert, however innocently, a strong sexual pull upon all the men of her "Coterie".

Who was to become "the Star of their Night" – their "Queen of the May" as the years rolled by. Also, did she not entertain them with her letters and her lavish hospitality? Make them feel important, at ease and never threatened? Offer constructive criticism of their work? That was Mrs Knight's secret. Her men friends were just that – friends and nothing more and they were happy to be dazzled without having to do anything about it.

All the members of the Coterie wrote poems in praise of Henrietta. Somervile presented her with a sonnet, one of many such verses she was to receive from her admirers.

As o'er Asteria's fields I rove,
Ten thousand beauties round me rise
And mingle pleasure with surprise.
By nature blest in every part
Adorned with every grace of art
This Paradise of blooming joys
Each raptured sense at once employs.

So he sets the scene – and then he poses the question:

Who formed this fair enchanting scene?

And to make sure that his message is clear, he encores the many beauties that have feasted his eye: "ye crystal floods", "ye breathing flowers", "ye shady woods", only to dismiss them "Your sweets decay, our verdures frown –", before the resolution of the poem in which he states:

"My soul's content on her alone" [10].

Surely a poem to please a lady. One that turns a pretty phrase and presents an elegant compliment. But he had plenty of competition. If Henrietta was Somervile's Asteria, she was William Shenstone's "Queen of the May", in a poem which expresses his joyful anticipation of a visit to Barrells:

When lo! in happier hour
I leave behind my native mead
To range where Zeal and Friendship lead,
To visit Luxborough's honoured bower [11].

Shenstone's friendship with Henrietta was to become close. He was to dominate many different aspects of her life, including her garden, her poetry and even her private life when he would be there – if needed – to offer support. The two were to encourage each other when experiencing the same kind of family problems and for a decade, at least, Mrs Knight was to see more of the poet than of anyone else. But that belongs to the future and for the present it is other members of the group who must take centre stage.

During those early days at Barrells, when this group of young men was busy with poetry to cast at the feet of their fair goddess, Jago wrote his pastoral, *Ardenna*. This was to take the form of an eclogue in praise of the ancient Forest of Arden, but at the same time could also be read as a celebration of Henrietta's beauty and of his friendship with her.

Then when from crowds the Loves and Graces flew
To these tone shades the beauteous maid withdrew
To study Nature in this calm retreat
And with confed'rate Art her charms compleat [12].

In spite of the less than fortunate "confed'rate" in line four, it presents a pretty compliment that the lady, herself, graciously acknowledges; "...you sir have the art to describe the most simple thing with the nicest elegance" [13], although by this time she must have been getting used to the many verses which continued to be strewn across her path. It is also of interest as the precursor to Jago's later verses such as "Blackbirds" which Shenstone was later to send to Robert Dodsley for inclusion in the latter's *Miscellanies* (Volume IV).

As the letters show, Henrietta received verses from Graves and Richard Whistler, too. The poems are lost, but it is clear that as well as paying Henrietta compliments they, as all the members of the Coterie, were anxious to obtain from her approbation for the literary work upon which they were embarked. Whistler's social satire, *The Shuttlecock*, she much enjoyed and it was not to be long before she was kept busy, "proof-reading" the many poems that were to find their way to Barrells (see Chapter 9).

But now it is time to return to the "father" of them all, Lord Somervile. As has been seen he was the oldest and earliest member of the Coterie, and when he died in 1742, Henrietta was to feel his loss keenly. He had, she writes, "till a few months (ago) retained all the vivacity of youth in his conversation": and had been, she tells Frances, "...the best friend and neighbour anyone could have [14]. Shenstone was also much saddened and writes from London of the squire who had enjoyed the good things of life; a profligate bon viveur who, as his debts mounted, had been obliged, "to drink himself into pain of the body in order to get rid of the pain of the mind" [15].

Somervile is buried in St Peter's Church, at Wootton Wawen in Warwickshire – in a tomb befitting the importance of his status as an aristocrat and Master of Foxhounds. A translation of its Latin inscription offers sound advice to his fellow church goers:

> *If thou hast found aught of good –*
> *imitate it,*
> *If aught of evil –*
> *avoid with all they strength;*
> *Trust in Christ and know that thou art*
> *Frail and mortal.*

His chief huntsman, John Hoitt, is also honoured here, with a memorial tablet that reminds us of a loyal servant and an appreciative master.

> *Here, Hoitt, all his sports and labours past*
> *Joins his loved master, Somervile at last.*

The inscription ends with a truism redolent of lines from the Grave Digger scene in "Hamlet".

> *Servant and Lord, when once we yield our breath*
> *Huntsman and poet are alike in death* [16].

Hamlet's musings reflect the same thoughts. This skull might be "of a courtier", or that of a "peasant". Such "that praised my Lord's horse when a meant to beg it". No matter to what social class we belong, we shall all end up "chopless" – to be knocked around by the Sexton's spade!

With the Coterie's support, and her self-esteem somewhat restored, Henrietta contrived to keep faith with her family, assuring her father upon his gift of a pint of citron water, that "every mark of your remembrance, be it in what shape so ever, is dear to me" [17]. This was while at home in Battersea, cracks were already appearing in the concrete of St John solidarity They had begun to show soon after Henrietta left when Lord St John had come to be persuaded, possibly by the Hertfords, that his daughter had been unjustly treated. It was a conclusion that decided him "to bar his door" to Robert Knight whom he now came to regard in a different light, He was not the only member of the family who began to have doubts. In June 1736, Bolingbroke was to solicit his brother-in-law in terms of strictest censure:

> *...when you not only decline the offer I make you... but,... put your son to school*
> *at Chelsea and your daughter to the worst you could have chose at Battersea, I*
> *protest to you, I am startled...* [18].

The spat was to die a natural death and the friendship of the two men survived; but one senses that from now on, Henrietta's brother became more wary, more circumspect in his dealings with Knight – and consequently more eager to fight his sister's battles. Later on, there is also to be evidence that Bolingbroke, too, began to feel that the family had reacted over hastily in their decision to banish Henrietta.

But in the long run, none of this altered Henrietta's situation very much; and that she could and did, on occasions, feel desperate is clear from an unheralded visit that she made to her friend, Frances, in August 1743.

The cause of the unhappiness that triggered such a move and prompted her to disobey her husband's injunction is not known, but it must have been something important, for she was not by nature the kind who would break her word.

That all was not well, was soon to be clear from her behaviour. Frances writes of it as being "light and giddy" – of her French way of dress and her "thoughtless manner". Writing to her son, Lord Beauchamp, she wittingly or not, paints a picture of an unhappy woman; one who is compensating for feelings of inadequacy and insecurity in a way which makes her revert to the youthful behaviour of happier days.

The visit was brief and does not seem to have diminished the future warmth of their friendship. However, it does serve to show how fragile the foundations were upon which Mrs Knight was obliged to rebuild her life. A new life made possible by her own courage and the warm esteem with which she came to be regarded by members of the "Coterie" – and kind neighbours – alike.

Chapter 8

THE WIDER CIRCLE

When winter was over, it was time for visiting and the Coterie did a great deal of that. At Ullenhall Henrietta was within reach of Snitterfield and Harbury where Jago was a parish priest. She was also near to Somervile at Edstone; Shenstone's Leasowes was not too far away and for Graves, further afield in Gloucestershire, a visit in the spring to Barrells was an acceptable ride for a young man on horseback. But Henrietta was to make new friends as well.

Through Shenstone she was to meet his brother, Joseph, a charming but sickly young man who had trained as an attorney in Bridgnorth but never practised: who was to come and live with the poet at the Leasowes – was less frugal with his money – and liked to discuss with Mrs Knight the new pamphlets and books that he had bought. She also met Maria, Shenstone's young cousin of whom "great things" were expected and whose untimely death, from smallpox, on a visit to London at the age of twenty-one, was to cause much grief.

Maria's father, the Reverend Thomas Dolman of Broome in Staffordshire, was Shenstone's uncle by marriage, and had opened his door to the two boys when their parents died. One of the poet's earliest memories, as he told Henrietta, was of the little village church with its bell set in a tree. This was rung by the parish clerk every Sunday in a ritual celebrated by Shenstone in an unpublished poem in praise of the music that it made:

Certes there are that hum a tune
And sing a song right well;
Yet sure no song was like my psalm
No music like my bell... [1]

Maria was to become a frequent visitor to Barrells as was Henrietta to the Dolman rectory at Broome – and the latter was quick to admire the conversation and musical prowess of this young girl so soon to be cut down in her prime.

It was through Shenstone that Mrs Knight was also to be introduced to the charming and easy-going Lord Dudley of The Grange in Halesowen – a mansion which is now a working men's club. This was a man who might seem an unlikely friend – for his education had been minimal; but he was convivial and would never miss an opportunity "to raise his glass". His toasts never varied, except by name, and in a letter to Henrietta from Shenstone he was to become "immortalized" for a nocturnal mishap recounted with relish:

> *My Lord Dudley has much irritated his great toe by hitting it against the bed's foot whilst he was strolling thro' the dark in full quest of the chamber pot* [2].

It is a trivial but amusing tale which elicits from Mrs Knight a light-hearted response. She is:

> *sorry Lord Dudley's toe has been so offended by his* **bed's foot**, *of which he should be cautious for the future, as I fear the damages would upon trial, fall on his Lordship than on that offender* [3].

John Scott Hylton, another of Shenstone's friends, was also to be introduced to Barrells. An engaging and enthusiastic young man, Hylton was to settle at Lapal House, now an old people's home, in Halesowen. But he found it difficult to relinquish London and to this end, had bought himself a place at Court for a thousand pounds – an enormous amount of money by to-day's standards. Not only was he rich – rich enough to berate "the money-getting slaves (who) think me mad to spend my life in idleness" [4], but he was also an engaging gossip, even, sadly, when this involved Henrietta's own daughter who caused a scandal by leaving her husband to elope with Sir Joshua Childs (see Chapter 15).

Then there was Morgan Graves, brother to Richard and heir to the Mickleton Estate. The elder brother was in the process of re-designing his garden after the manner of a distant relative, Philip Southcote – whose ideas were also to encourage Shenstone into attempting so successfully a similar project at the Leasowes. In his turn, the poet was to oversee much of the work carried out in Henrietta's garden, so a direct line can be traced via Richard Graves to Morgan, to Shenstone and to Mrs Knight.

An interest in gardening was to provide a link with some of Henrietta's aristocratic neighbours, including Lord and Lady Plymouth of Hewell Grange, and Lord and Lady Archer of Umberslade Hall. Visits to the latter were to be quite frequent and Henrietta tells Shenstone of an invitation to be shown their new obelisk from the "saloon", so that she can "better judge how it appears".

Lord Archer seems to have been a kind hearted man, enquiring after Shenstone's Leasowes which he understands is "the prettiest and most elegant place in all these parts"[5]: a message which Mrs Knight lost little time in relaying to her friend. Upon his death, Lord Archer was to become the victim of an infamous lampoon, written in the form of a "mock" epitaph which circulated at the time:

Here lies Lord Archer
Whose insignificance protected him while living, even from contempt, His mind was unacquainted with any sentiment that might have dignified the meanest of his companions, Whom he selected from the most wretched of mortals...

So it continues and it is with relief that we pass on from the unfortunate gentleman's "boorish vulgarity", and his "natural stupidity" to the end of this unkind nonsense which postulates that:

(he) died, unlamented, in the honourable exercise of basket making[6].

What, one wonders, could the poor man have done, to engender such venom, spite and vindictiveness?

The friendship of local gentry like the Archers and the Plymouths demonstrates that when Mrs Knight came to live at Barrells, she was not spurned by all the members of her own class as received opinion would have it. Some did not open their doors, and some like Mrs Dews, the sister of Mrs Delaney, were cautious. Mrs Dews had recently moved from Gloucestershire to Shipston-upon-Stour, and in 1750, was to write to her sister for advice. Should Henrietta's offer of friendship be accepted or declined? The response is interesting:

Now for Lady Luxborough. I am vastly entertained at your being acquainted with her in spite of your prudence, but I really see no reason why her acquaintance is to be declined. If she leads a discreet life, and does generous and charitable things, she ought to be taken notice of, as an encouragement to go on in the path, and your conversation and example may be of infinite service to her. She has lively parts, is **very well bred** *and knows the polite world, and you may, I think, divert yourself with her as much as you can, and D.D. says you will only do a meritorious thing in so doing* [7].

All this may sound rather "superior" to us today, but so was the friendship condoned and one can only hope that Henrietta was to find the resultant intimacy rewarding. It does not seem likely, for Mrs Dews, even then, was not very enthusiastic, and while Henrietta writes of her pleasure in "seeing Mrs Dews three times" while she is staying in Mappleborough Green for a change of air; the latter is describing Lady Luxborough in less than flattering terms. Because of bad weather:

We were obliged to ask leave of Lady Luxborough to come through her grounds, the roads being so bad the other way a coach cannot come. She was at the door to receive us, and obliged me to go in, was most profoundly civil, and comes to see me this week;…

But she is "not vastly fond of her acquaintance, though she is entertaining and has made her house and garden very pretty" [8].

Fortunately there were other women friends whose loyalty was beyond reproach. 1750 was the year when Mrs Dews first came on the scene; by which time Mrs Holyoake had been holding out the hand of friendship for well over a decade. Mrs Davis and Mrs Kendall, two ladies from Stratford-upon-Avon, were also to give Henrietta support – especially the former, who with her Ladyship spent much time transcribing Shenstone's poetry.

Upon reflection, the circle can be further widened to include the Lytteltons of Hagley Hall, Henrietta's brother Bolingbroke who gets a chapter to himself, and Robert Dodsley who was a friend of William Shenstone. Dodsley, the footman turned publisher, playwright and poet; whose name in the eighteenth century was to become as familiar as those of Dr Johnson and David Garrick. It was to Dodsley's popular Volume IV of his *Miscellanies* of poetry that each member of the Coterie was to contribute.

Finally there is Henrietta's secretary, the well-liked and urbane Mr Outing. That members of the Coterie approved of him is clear – he was frequently invited to join Shenstone and Jago on their visits to London where by all accounts he presented a different face. Here he would make free with his weapon and on one occasion "...laid his hand upon his sword six times and threatened a dozen men (with) death, one of whom was Broughton, the prize fighter"[9]. Not, one would think, a very sensible thing to do!

In his professional capacity Outing was at the centre of Henrietta's world. It is a world that we glimpse through the eyes of her friends and especially those of her Coterie. For these were a group of men remarkable, not so much for their literary achievements which were considerable; (Shenstone's *The Schoolmistress* is a literary gem and Grave's novel *The Spiritual Quixote*, a gentle satire upon the rise of the Methodist Movement, is still admired today) but for their letters, not least Henrietta's own, with their store of primary source material. In these is mapped a country at once foreign and familiar. Brought vividly before us are the sights and customs – the recorded conversations of life on a screen that has flickered and died.

Outing, the Coterie and a widening circle. A world in which Henrietta was to wear her charm and her wit with distinction. Now a very different woman to the one she had left behind in London; one who in spite of life's challenges was to reign as "Queen of the May" for some time to come.

Chapter 9

BARRELLS HOUSE
AND GARDEN

In spite of its rather grand name, Barrells Hall at the time of Henrietta's arrival was an ancient and dilapidated farmhouse of modest proportions. Mrs Knight, it will be remembered, had found it "without doors or windows", and it is not surprising that a considerable sum of money had to be spent to make it "now very habitable".

Although he refused to meet with her, "it can never be proper that we should ever meet again in this world", Robert Knight had assured his wife that "I shall willingly pay for any conveniences you are desirous of to make Barrells a comfortable habitation"[1]. But his willingness was to come at a price. It meant that he could, did and would meddle in his wife's affairs. And why, one is obliged to ask, did he wait until the house was occupied before instigating repairs to roof, windows and doors?

Mr Knight was liberal with his advice. He was against replacing the pitted walnut wainscot in the "Great Parlor" until the view from its windows was improved and "the farmyard is laid out into a kitchen garden"[2]. He specified the number of servants that his wife might employ. "It appears that Smith, the Cook, the Laundry Maid and the Country House Maid will be necessary... the others you may spare"[3]. Permission to keep two men servants, James and – John "who is able to drive a Coach and the Chaise in the French manner"[4] was granted, but not the coachman who was to be discharged "on or before Michaelmas". So with every stroke of his pen, is Robert Knight the epitome of an all powerful eighteenth century husband, confident that his behaviour is resultant upon duty.

Sometimes it pleased him to be generous. Henrietta was permitted to have furniture sent down from London. But sometimes he was less inclined to look favourably upon his wife's endeavours. In 1742, her debts spiralled and his response to her plea for aid was penned in the third person. "Lord Luxborough recommends to Lady Luxborough to reduce immediately the number of her Servants and Horses by one half" [5].

On this occasion it is possible that however unfortunately expressed, his exasperation, was justified. For there can be no denying that her Ladyship was profligate with money. "...nor could I ever be forced" she tells Shenstone, "even by experience" and she certainly had enough of that, "into a proper **veneration for sixpence**"; citing as justification the very human aspiration that "to eat one's cake when one is ahungered, is most sweet" [6]. So it was in this frame of mind that she came to devise grand plans for her house and garden to which her enjoyable visits to see Shenstone at the Leasowes gave increased momentum.

That she well understood the pecuniary problems that her ambitions would precipitate is clear:

> *Nor should I have ventured a visit to the Leasowes, where the more one sees the more one admires, and that admiration leads towards envy, which as a hermitess I ought to shun* [7].

And with particular reference to the garden:

> *I have talked of nothing but the beauty of Virgil's Grove and the meanness of my own, which used to give me some pleasure, but is (now) so much lessened in my esteem* [8].

It is a very human reaction and one with which many can empathise. And it demonstrates how inevitable it was that Henrietta should turn to her friend for guidance, both in the improvement of her house and in the design of her garden. For had he not wrestled with the same problems? Was not his farmstead also of modest proportions? And was he not also constantly looking for ways to create an illusion of space in his home – as by the judicious positioning of mirrors where downstairs in his parlour:

> *At the other end of the chamber, a door led into a favourite front room from where "visto fashion" could be seen a hint of the Clent Hills, a view enhanced by its reflection in a suitably placed pier glass opposite* [9].

Or by more structural means such as the knocking of two rooms into one (which then measured nineteen feet by twelve): or by the use of stone coloured stucco wallpaper throughout to create uniformity.

All these innovations were noted by Henrietta who, like Shenstone, was anxious to make the most of the individual potential of each and every room. As a means of creating more living space she has "turned a dairy into a library", a room "which I chiefly inhabit"; and one with a ceiling so low, she explains to Lady Hertford, that "I can almost touch, (it)..." But she is pleased that, even so, there is just sufficient room to hang "your Ladyship's pictures" [10].

On a further occasion and at Shenstone's instigation, Henrietta had the chimney breast in her study moved twelve inches to create symmetry, and was subsequently obliged to compromise in her efforts to accommodate the poet's grandiloquent advice concerning its subsequent decoration. Shenstone had suggested woodcarvings of "Lyres, Laurels, Fistulas, Pipes, Masks etc. united by a kind of Bandage falling easily down to the Wainscott" [11]. But in the end it all seemed rather grand for a room "only hung with sixpenny paper... so low that I have but five inches between Pope's Head and the motto over it" [12]. In the end she opted instead for "my friend Williams" to paint the same ornamentation in relief "in stone colours to appear like carving" [13].

As a further means of decoration and always with an eye to fashion, she toyed with the idea of lead carving "which ladies do themselves by cutting ... thin lead with scissors, and shaping it into flowers, knots etc. and fixing it to wire" [14]. But decided against it.

Later, in 1752, she was to create a new bedroom and dressing room and it was around this time that she became interested in another fashionable craze – papier-maché – to decorate the ceiling of her "grand parlor". Shenstone volunteered where she could obtain the material, "from Mr Bromwich at the Golden Lion upon Ludgate Hill"; and he explained that for a ceiling of this size she would require "an ornament for the middle and four spandrels for the corners" [15]. So that she could see what this would look like, he even took down his own paper-maché "pineapple" centre-piece and sent it to her, complete with corner ornaments.

The library, study, great parlor, bedroom and hall in which by the early seventeen fifties:

> *The Doric Pediment is begun; and a little alteration… is completed which will show the intended pediment to some advantage within doors* [16].

Each show how, little by little, with loving care and attention to detail Henrietta over many years was to renovate and transform her tumble down shell of a house into a gracious home.

But this home, certainly much admired, was only a piece of the jigsaw that would remain unfinished until, out of a wilderness, was created her delightful garden. A garden which for the first years of her exile, she was to tackle without Shenstone's help for the two did not meet until 1739 – a fact which means that what she did and when, is open to speculation. There is also the problem of those missing letters. From 1742 to 1747, there is a gap in Henrietta's collected letters to Shenstone, so for information one is obliged to turn elsewhere – to Lady Hertford in fact.

But to return to Mrs Knight's garden in the 1730's. With two aims in view: to improve the outlook from the "grand parlor" as her husband had suggested, and to provide food for the household, one of Henrietta's earliest tasks was to replace the old fashioned farmyard that she had inherited, with a well-stocked kitchen garden. Fresh soft fruit in the summer and vegetables for most of the year – that was her ambition. It was a first big step soon to be followed by others, for by the time that Shenstone appeared on the scene the wilderness scythed, cut down and tamed around the house, presented open green spaces where visitors might sit – where the poet **did** sit with William Somervile one balmy evening beneath the famous Barrells' double oak.

From then on Shenstone would lead the way. He would show Mrs Knight how she might emulate at Barrells what he had achieved so successfully at the Leasowes. Show her how, by creating new vistas and opening up views, the farm, the garden and surrounding countryside could blend into a perfect whole. The aim was to create a "modern" natural looking garden in which artifice, or which there was a good deal, must remain hidden. A fact that Henrietta well understood, as is clear from some lines that she penned while on a visit to Shenstone's Leasowes in 1749:

> *'Tis Nature here makes pleasing scenes arise,*
> *And wisely gives them Shenstone to revise,*
> *To veil each flaw, to brighten every grace,*
> *Yet still to let them wear their parent's face* [17].

These were the precepts also to be adopted by Henrietta and it is not surprising that she should point out, "If anything is done here (at Barrells), it will be owing to the advice you are so kind to give me" [18]. Writing to Lady Hertford in 1742, she described what some of these innovations were. They included:

> *...a garden which I am filling with all the flowering shrubs I can get. I have made an aviary and filled it with a variety of singing birds, and am now making a fountain in the middle of it, and a grotto to sit and hear them sing, contiguous to it. This, as it is seen from the window of the houses, affords me some amusement. And in a coppice a little further I have made a very lovely cave shaded by trees...* [19].

It was to Shenstone that Henrietta turned when contemplating a screen to provide her with more privacy "from the cottage that is contiguous to my garden" [20] and which was eventually to be constructed in the form of an ornamental wall and seat. It was a project to be followed by the building of a small pedimented pavilion. This was much altered before completion because she kept on changing her mind, but eventually it was to house a shrine to Venus and be positioned "to terminate in a row of trees on a green fronting the door of my house" [21]. Over many months she writes to Shenstone of its progress until triumphantly – "My pavilion is finished all to tiling and flooring" [22]. And later, "Mr Outing has put *O Venus Reginci Giridi* in the new pavilion over Venus's Shrine..." [23].

So it was a great disappointment when Mr Hall – perpetual curate at Henley and a favourite of the Circle – volunteered when taking tea one day with Henrietta that he felt the roof of the new building to be "...too low!" For as she was quick to point out to Shenstone, "If it had been any higher ... my house would have appeared lower than my pavilion" [24], and her aim, to enhance her home and its environs would have been frustrated. Which only goes to show that one does not always obtain the response that one would like, that perhaps it is better to play safe and not to ask!

At any rate, Henrietta's pavilion, whether the correct height or not, was completed during the summer of 1749. Its construction had taken eighteen months and it was in fact one of a number of ongoing schemes with which she was to become involved; some of which were to include general landscaping of quite vast areas. There was for example, the shrubbery.

Shrubberies only look their best at certain times of the year, and the late summer of 1748 was a time when her Ladyship could refer wittily to her garden as a "Ferme negligée"; when "the roses (are)... all faded, and give an ugly aspect to my shrubbery, which awaits your (Shenstone's) directions to be new modelled" [25]. These, it turned out, came quick and fast and the poet's long distance advice which poured forth in a paper stream from the Leasowes was not always understood. It was not long before Henrietta has her doubts as to:

whether I rightly understand in what manner you would have the Hermitage become part of the shrubbery, by means of about three yards of shrubbery on the outside of my lime walk? [26]

But soon she is thanking him for "your little sketch of alterations in my shrubbery" and losing no time in implementing his suggestions which she has come to view as a joint operation. She is also in the process of "taking down styles that no foot road may prevent the execution of what *we* propose" [27].

At the same time she is embarking upon other major improvements. She has transformed her lower garden by merging a series of smaller plots into a single grassed area. Her upper garden has been turned into a bowling green and her "court" by which she means her "driveway" has been extended, raised and gravelled. This was soon to be "honoured with Mrs Kendall's coach and six" [28], a most opulent equipage which was to find "room sufficient" for parking and thus vindicate all the hard work and expense. The visit was to give her Ladyship much satisfaction and one is reminded of that time at the Leasowes when Henrietta's coach with its newly painted coronet made a first visit there. It was in 1745, soon after Mrs Knight had metamorphosed into Lady Luxborough and Shenstone wrote to Richard Jago of his thrill of pleasure at her arrival. "A coach with a coronet is a pretty Kind of Phaenomenon at my Door; few Things prettier..." [29]. The baptism of Henrietta's driveway by the Kendall coach and six would have induced a similar warm glow of pride.

It was around this time, in the June of 1749, that a ha-ha was under construction at Barrells. Her Ladyship does not bother herself with the minutiae of the operations – merely recording "The Hah Hah! is digging". But its purpose, to provide without obscuring the view, a boundary to prevent farm animals from encroaching into the garden area, presents an opportunity to consider Henrietta's other role – that of farmer. For her Ladyship embraced country life with enthusiasm – churning cheese in her dairy to send to her brother Bolingbroke, "the best cheese" he responded "I ever ate".

Then there was her poultry. In the eighteenth century, the raising of poultry was considered an occupation sufficiently "genteel" even for ladies and Henrietta was proud of her turkeys, her guinea fowl and her hens. In the summer of 1749, she ruefully tells of a polecat which "fetched away twenty (turkeys) in one night and eight at three in the afternoon next day" [30]. Amusingly, her Ladyship blames herself for being too pleased with her own endeavours, "punished for my presumption in daring all my neighbours to produce such fine turkeys as mine, of which I had thirty-seven" [31]. On one occasion Henrietta sends Shenstone eight guinea fowl eggs for his supper – rather many, one would have thought for a single meal. On another, she makes him a present of a pair of very fine geese.

> *Don Pedro who has all the stateliness of a swan and Donna Elvira his faithful consort who has filled my vallies with complaint for the long summer days* [32].

The impression is again of her Ladyship's adaptability – of her determination to make the most of a kind of life she did not choose but from which she was to reap much reward.

Back in the garden Henrietta planted a row of white poplars (abeles), along a lane beside her coppice. She constructed a summerhouse with "plasterwork by John Wright of Worcester" and planted a lime avenue. Then there was her thatched hermitage erected in a location described by Shenstone as "preferable to any in England"; a sundial and gates to enclose her driveway (court) – and much more which if detailed, could make the list read like an estate agent's brochure. And as Shenstone had done, she provided benches and turf seats, strategically placed where visitors were encouraged to enjoy a view of her garden or beyond as far as Oldberrow Church or the hamlet of Skilts several miles away.

There were other less appealing similarities between life at Barrells and at the Leasowes. Henrietta had problems with trespassers who used her coppice and her service walk as short cuts to Henley.

> *There is no keeping the people out of the Service Walk; they come through the neighbouring Coppice into the Lane, and from thence over my hedge that is on the bank, which they have broke down in forty places, and so into the service road and away...* [33].

With Shenstone, the problem was locals who picked and uprooted wild flowers planted in Virgil's Grove, who caused havoc as they tramped down his delicate plants. Henrietta's dilemma was solved by the ingenuity of her new Scottish gardener, Mr Hume. He built another ha-ha, followed by a "high bank across the lane", so turning the temptation of sneaking a short cut into an impenetrable obstacle race.

The poet was to solve his dilemma by means of a delicious little poem, *In Cool Grot,* composed over breakfast one morning and "posted" on the side of a roothouse in his Grove. In it he tells his readers that they have now entered a magical place.

> *Here in cool grot and mossy cell*
> *We rural fays and fairies dwell.*

He advises that plants should be treated with care. Visitors must –

> *…Tread with awe these favoured bowers*
> *Nor wound the shrubs, nor bruise the flowers;*

Finally comes the warning in the last couplet:

> *But harm betide the wayward swain*
> *Who dares our hallowed haunts profane* [34].

As Shenstone humorously explained when he sent the verses to Henrietta; the lines were written

> *For the admonition of my good Friends, the Vulgar, of whom I have Multitudes every Sunday evening and who very fortunately believe in fairies and are no judge of poetry* [35].

Good verse or not, the lines were effective. The pilfering stopped and the poet had every reason to feel satisfied.

In spite of problems like these there were also great benefits from living in the country. Henrietta writes of springtime in the garden, a time which "shews at least the beauties of childhood", when there are "plenty of snowdrops, primroses, polyanthus, and even violets"[36]. She writes of her joy at the first "cowslips, ragged robins, wild hyacinths"; and in her shrubbery of Whitsun roses and syringa which now replaces her lilac.

It was in the spring, in an improved and enlarged kitchen garden for which Shenstone must take the credit, that her Ladyship planted her seeds: melon and lettuce from her brother Bolingbroke, Spanish Broom which "my gardener designs to raise..."; and that "greatest curiosity" of a flower which the world provides, a plant which has "a pod as big as a pineapple and perfumes a room even when not in flower"[37]. This was a gift from her neighbour, Parson Hall, who "has also got me a water-engine of lignium vitae which will water my garden with much ease"[38]. Such were the technical triumphs of the eighteenth century. On another occasion we come across Henrietta collecting seeds to send to Shenstone. In a charming portrayal of domesticity she explains how "Mr Outing and I are gathering flower seeds proper for your (Shenstone's) grove, among them some Star of Bethlehem and Passion Flowers"[39].

And always, whether seed collecting, tree planting or re-designing large swathes of garden, there was more to do; but for some period of time, nothing seems to have occupied her so intensively as the purchasing, design and placement of a memorial urn to her great friend, William Somervile. Shenstone was instructed by means of a vague imperative to "pray think of a place to set the urn in"[40], while in the meantime her Ladyship and Outing searched "every corner of the coppice and (could) find no oak favourable"[41]. Success at last was to be provided by the Barrells' famous double oak where after many letters and much consultation it was "erected this morning" where it "now makes a good Figure under its Canopy"[42] no doubt to the relief of all concerned.

To the end of her life Henrietta continued to lavish time, thought and money – certainly money – upon her home and her garden. "What an immense deal" writes Shenstone, "it must have cost to fit up an House (and garden) in the manner you have done at Barrells"[43]. So it is no surprise that she frequently overstretched her finances. In order to pay for some of her schemes she was obliged to sell family jewels left to her by her brother, Hollis. It is also suggested that she sold a quantity of silver tableware as well. From 1745 onwards, her servants' wages posed a problem and sometimes they were not paid at all. Promises were made... but it has to be said that these were not always kept and Lord Luxborough's exasperated:

> *Can it be said for the credit of any person to drive with a coach and six horses,*
> *when the wages of the stewards who attend that equipage are unpaid...* [44].

Is one of the few valid comments that he made.

From Lady Luxborough's point of view, things would have been seen differently. In many ways she was a good and caring employer (see Chapter 10), and her garden – it must be remembered – had become her life's work. Plans had taken on a momentum of their own, encouraged, not only by Shenstone, but by wealthy neighbours like the Plymouths and the Archers, aristocrats with whose grandiose schemes she could not compete.

So when the wealthy James West of Alscot Park, near Stratford, not only came to view Barrells but approved so much of what he saw that he despatched his gardener to garner any "tips" for use back home, Henrietta's delight was palpable. "The great Mr West of the Treasury sent his gardener today to view my small Garden and my Walks" [45], she writes excitedly to Shenstone the minute her visitor had left.

Her Ladyship's garden became widely known and well visited and provided her with fresh air, exercise and peace of mind. In it she found the serenity that, years earlier, she had been obliged to forfeit, and even when dogged by ill health, would walk "my usual round of Gardens and Coppice" [46] whenever she could.

The creation of an elegant home and a garden of imaginative flair was a success story to which many with lesser determination, less adaptability and imagination could not have aspired. It was also to provide a marvellous backdrop to her other, equally successful undertakings: her social and literary interests which are to be the subjects of further chapters.

The Rotunda, Ranelagh Gardens, by Canaletto.

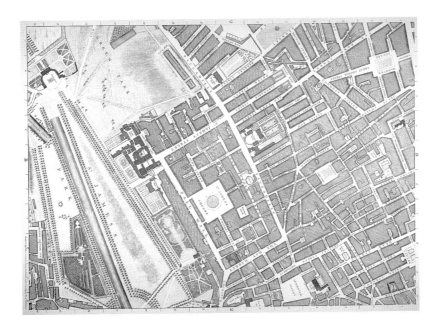

Detail of a map from The A to Z of Georgian London, by John Rocque, c.1746.

IX

Alexander Pope, by William Hoare.

John Gay, by William Aikman, c.1729.

George Frideric Handel, by William Bromley; Thomas Hudson.

Ralph Allen, by John Faber Jr; Thomas Hudson.

Samuel Richardson, by Joseph Highmore.

Henry Fielding, by William Hogarth.

William Shenstone, by Edward Alcock.

William Somervile, artist unknown.

Richard Graves, by Samuel William Reynolds, from an engraving by James Northcote.

Richard (Beau) Nash, artist unknown.

Spernal Church and Parsonage. Drawing by James Saunders, c.1810.

Ullenhall Chapel. Drawing by James Saunders, c.1810.

Beaudesert Church. Drawing by James Saunders, c.1810.

Chapter 10

LADY LUXBOROUGH'S LETTERS TO WILLIAM SHENSTONE

Nowhere is Henrietta's personality more vividly portrayed than in her letters from Barrells to William Shenstone. From them it is clear, not only that she was perceptive and witty – but that she was lonely. Exile at Barrells may have had its compensations, even provided her with moments of considerable pleasure, but it exacted a heavy toll. She writes of friendship, "the conversation of a chosen few that smoothes the rugged road of life"[1]. She tells of her delight in autumn and her apprehension of winter, "the frozen solitary season that approaches"[2]. In them we read about her garden, or travel back with her to her youthful London days. We are introduced to her extended "family" of servants – share her thoughts about eighteenth century novelists. These letters read like a map of her Ladyship's life and opinions.

Winter was a time when local roads, usually little more than dirt tracks, were frequently impassable; a time when the "hermitess" of Barrells was even more dependent, as was Shenstone, upon the correspondence of friends. Cut off from her London intimates and the gaiety of Court life, Mrs Knight as she then was, spent many hours penning her letters – for "selfish" reasons so that she might obtain her reward, a "packet" in response. She wrote from her chimney corner, at her writing table and even, quite frequently, in bed: and in spite of protestations to the contrary, the exquisitely crafted and sometimes beautifully illustrated letters that arrived at Shenstone's door were the result of much hard work.

At a time when the post was uncertain, the safe arrival of letters was suspect and people were frequently obliged to make their own arrangements. On occasion, Henrietta would use Frankie Holyoake's enterprising and privately run postal service; or "Colliers belonging to Halesowen, who pretend to be well acquainted with the Leasowes"[3]; or more desperately, any tradesman who "happened" to be heading in that direction. When all else failed she would send her servant, Joe, as Shenstone employed his "trusty Tom" – both men who could be relied upon to wait and bring home a reply.

But the "exquisite pleasure" of the arrival of letters was counter-balanced by "anxious fear" when delay might signal illness, loss or even the suspicion of having given offence. The dread of losing a friend was one that Henrietta expressed frequently and yet she was not above rebuking the poet if she felt that he had been dilatory in not responding promptly. Even so, friendship is precious. It is about feeling comfortable with people; a relationship which means that all "...ceremony vanishes".

Both friends are proud of the letters they receive. Henrietta believes that the poet gives:

Innocent pleasure to yourself and instruction as well as pleasure to others, by the amusements you follow. Your pen, your pencil, your taste... give such an example, as it were wished might be generally followed – few have the capacity... to spend their time so usefully, as well as unblameably... [4].

Responding, Shenstone maintains that Henrietta "can make letters shine by Dint of Genius" – that she has not need of the trappings of gilt paper and exotic seals to "sell" their content; and her handwriting, "which has all the firmness of a Man's hand with all the delicacy of a Female's"[5] is a fitting vehicle for her thoughts.

Whilst correspondence perpetuated their friendship, it was visits to each other that cemented it. Much to Shenstone's delight, when her estranged husband was elevated to the peerage in 1742, Mrs Knight became Lady Luxborough. As has been seen (see Chapter 9) her newly emblazoned coach arriving at the Leasowes was an event which he records with evident satisfaction: "...a pretty kind of phaenomenon. Few things prettier"[6].

But such outward display of new found status did little to remedy her Ladyship's isolation. She graced a few more dinner tables, but except for members of her household, Henrietta would frequently see nobody for days at a time. This is why she looked forward so much to planning, paying and receiving visits.

Her letters are punctuated with invitations. "I depend upon your promise of coming soon to Barrells" [7] she entreats and later, "social Winter will vie not only with fruitful Autumn but also with flowering Spring... if you favour my Hermitage with your company" [8]. But Shenstone was a difficult man with whom to negotiate and to determine upon a date with the poet who believed that "fixing days is an encroachment upon liberty" [9], must surely have been a problem! She was frequently disappointed and a crie-de-coeur from her pen at such a time: "Whether you are alive or dead... remember that you have a sincere friend... impatient for the pleasure of your company" [10], tells of her frustration. One summer, in an attempt to encourage the poet she pens an entrancing portrait of a summer evening at Barrells where she sits beneath a canopy of oak, "looking at the neighbouring hills, hearing my mowers whet their scythes (and) seeing the troop horses scamper about my avenue" [11].

Unfortunately with little result. But when Shenstone **was** persuaded to commit himself, and whether he came alone or brought a friend, he was always a delightful and appreciative guest. At the harpsichord he would play and sing – he had an attractive, light tenor voice; or at table read his poems. His was a silken tongue and conversation flowed. It was at times like this that Henrietta would have been reminded of those early days when as a younger woman she was a guest at her brother Bolingbroke's estate at Dawley (see Chapter 11). More importantly, the poet knew how to please and would leave behind an appreciative note or verse for his hostess to find when he had left:

How pleased we pass the Winter's day
And charm the dull-eyed spleen away [12].

He understood that the pangs of leave taking were acutely felt. "Nothing is so terrible as parting from friends" opines Henrietta and on another occasion: "friends and neighbours combine to leave me at once to solitude and regret" [13].

One episode illustrates vividly her Ladyship's vulnerability. In 1751 an invitation to visit on her birthday had elicited from the poet no response: "As I did not hear from you I concluded every minute you was just coming" [14] she records in words pregnant with anticipation. Several unanswered letters later, she paints a bitter-sweet picture of how the day came to be spent – alone, save for Captain Robinson and his troop horses. The same gentleman sufficiently gallant to serenade her with his "German flute" and later on his bagpipes "...whilst we (members of her household) bowled and had our syllabub out of doors" [15].

Instead of the company of an intimate friend she had been obliged to rely upon the kindness of a comparative stranger, albeit one with whom "...it was a pleasure to converse" and who admired Henrietta's urn in memory of Somervile, a sure way to her heart! But he was not Shenstone. And her plea – "I never had so much occasion for your company and your letters which I find a relish in (as I do now)" [16], would have to wait several weeks before an answer. Then the poet's eventual response buoyed her spirits. It transpired that he had been busy supervising workmen on his farm; and his "Masons and Carpenters! The Lord deliver me", was to provide a satisfactory reason for his non-appearance. And his genuine concern for her "Depression of spirits of which you so seldom complain" [17], demonstrated an empathy which only an intimate might feel. Henrietta was reassured.

This need for reassurance was felt by both and can be seen on many occasions in the way the friends supported each other. That same year, when the poet's brother died and Shenstone's heart "is well nigh broke", her Ladyship's response, "your grief for your brother I feel in its full force" [18], was reinforced by action. Her own brother Bolingbroke had also recently died and she understood. She sent her servant, Joe, to the Leasowes with a packet of "toys" – buckles and buttons of the sort he enjoyed collecting.

The friends had other problems in common. In the 1750's Shenstone was embroiled in a legal battle over Harborough Hall (the family home of Shenstone's mother) with his nephew, young Dolman: "...this little fellow who may well have malignity enough to cut my throat"[19]. At this time her Ladyship's troubles also centred around property. Having restored her home and transformed it into an elegant dwelling, she confides that now both her husband and son-in-law have designs upon it – that she must "keep garrison at Barrells" and dare not meet with them unless a solicitor is present.

Such perceptions colour her letters. Resentment at treatment by a husband unwilling to believe in her innocence and society over eager to pronounce her guilt, frequently flares and her overriding concern is that her thoughts and actions should not be misinterpreted. She has "suffered too much" to risk again "unjust censure"; worries lest "my ill fortune reaches my friends" and looks forward to visiting the Leasowes where "ingratitude and malice" do not penetrate.

But to dwell upon Henrietta's loneliness and periodic unhappiness is to present a one-sided picture, for she was born with a vivacity and love of life that enabled her to overcome her misfortunes at least as frequently as she succumbed to them. When she is happy, the letters sparkle with her zest for life. Then, her "hand and pen being upon the gallop"[20], even the inconsequential is imbued with interest. She enthuses about her garden, writes of her friends and neighbours with perception and wit.

Henrietta had many caring neighbours and the letters present charming vignettes of country life. We read of her chaplain, Parson Holyoake, and his friend Jackie Reynolds, playing bowls by moonlight. Of Parson Allen, whose passion for whist and mince pies made him, every Christmas, "forget his friends and every... duty beyond... his parish"[21]. Who on one occasion so enjoyed a visit to Barrells that he "Kept me up till three (am) to hear his stories"[22]. We read of the Henley Bellman who "has gone his Christmas round"; and of Shenstone's servant, Tom, arriving to find her Ladyship in the middle of consuming a large barrel of oysters with her friends, the Holyoakes. Small wonder that digestive problems were so frequent at this time! We are introduced to the Meredith family who "act plays sometimes at home". And especially to Miss Patty whose Ophelia so entrances Shenstone and who because "she does some of the mad parts... very finely"[23], is persuaded to "do a scene or two" when staying with her Ladyship.

Mrs Meredith was Henrietta's cousin and the family had never wavered in its support. Their amateur dramatics involved the whole household and their productions, undertaken enthusiastically, are redolent of Jane Austen's *Mansfield Park*. They have scenery from the "Playhouse", and make proper "stage dresses" and invite their friends to join the audience. There is even talk on one occasion of taking their production to London!

Henrietta reminisces about the gilded world of her youth. She tells of her parents' friendship with George I. Of the King's partiality for apricots stewed in brandy which he first tasted at their Battersea home – and of the subsequent annual presents of this delicacy to his Majesty by her "mama". She writes amusingly of the year when apricots were scarce and their number correspondingly less; of the King's way of economising by eating the *same* amount but on *alternate* nights. Her ladyship tells of "the great Handel" who told her that inspiration for some of his "best songs" came from cries of street vendors marketing their wares. She remembers the day that she "stole" a gilt picture frame belonging to the future Queen Caroline.

The friends loved to gossip. They write of their servants who in both establishments were part of an extended family – and who in Henrietta's case, replaced the London family that she had "lost". We are introduced to Mrs Lane, her Ladyship's housekeeper, whose good opinion Shenstone is keen to foster. To her counterpart, the poet's much loved Mrs Arnold. "I enquired of your man after Mrs Arnold", writes Henrietta. "If he does not tell her, pray let this letter say, I am her hearty well wisher" [24].

Then there was her Ladyship's Joe who could translate French into English and who delivered her package of "toys" to Shenstone with such "great care and Expedition". There was the poet's "trusty Tom" who had an excellent head for business and whose gardening skills, especially the building of his little moss seats and root houses, were frequently in demand at Barrells.

Much was inconsequential as is the story of Hannah, Shenstone's scullery maid, and the fruitless attempts to discover who had sent her a valentine. Some was of more concern as when her Ladyship's old retainer, Mr Price, was taken mortally ill. Unable to climb the stairs, he was transferred to a guest room on the first floor at Barrells where he was attended by none other than Dr Wall of Worcester, Henrietta's own consultant physician.

Henrietta's concern for the well being of her staff was paramount; and whilst, sadly, it is true that they were not always regularly paid, equally so, their welfare was never neglected. The story of Hannah's sister is one among many. The girl was employed as a dairymaid at Barrells where the rigours of the job were to prove too severe. Mr Holyoake, her Ladyship's doctor, was to diagnose rheumatism exacerbated by cold and rain, "a great misfortune to a servant and makes it impossible to a mistress to keep one so tender" [25]. It was a situation which called for the immediate summoning of her Ladyship's post chaise in which the girl was transported safely back to the Leasowes and the care of her sister.

Both friends were keen to be kept in touch with the London social scene and regale each other with stories told by friends. Henrietta tells of Vauxhall ladies who "crow like cocks" to attract attention of a likely looking young man. Shenstone of the Pantin, "a sort of Scaramouch which ladies bring into company" [26], a life sized cardboard puppet by means of which they communicated.

Henrietta loves to discuss literature. Shenstone frequently asks for advice about his poems and together they discuss Pope whose "peevish little Mind" her Ladyship dislikes. But she admires Fielding "who cannot write without humour"; whose *Tom Jones* with its far-fetched plot is redeemed by his portrayal of "good" characters as if in a "concave glass which discovers blemishes that would not have appeared to the common eye" [27]. On the other hand, Henrietta's' interest in Smollett's *Roderick Random*, a novel she dislikes, is because a childhood companion, the now notorious Lady Vane (see Personalia), has managed to get her Memoirs incorporated as a chapter in Volume II. Her Ladyship is scandalized:

Published by her own order, from her own Memoirs, given to the author for that purpose; and by approbation of her own Lord. What was equal to that fact? [28]

Henrietta's disapproval spills on to the page and one wonders whether she would have reacted in this way, if she really had been "guilty" of an indiscretion all those years ago?

Nearer to home, the friends discuss the **theory** of "oeconomy" if not its practice – possibly because both were improvident and had little appetite for reform. "I hope" writes Henrietta, that "you will give me rules for "oeconomy", adding wickedly: "...even though you may know the theory better than the practice" [29]. And she is delighted with the poet's analogy of his unsuccessful endeavours to retrench. His situation is like a "Butterdish with a spout at both ends or the sluice of a Pond which lets out twice as much as comes in" [30].

They both have problems with rent collecting. Whilst her Ladyship bemoans her lack of enthusiasm for the job, Shenstone volunteers that one of his tenants, six months in arrears, will not commit himself to repayment because he has no wish to break a promise! Hilarity escalates... although ultimately Henrietta admits that a little frugality would be "very wholesome" – before carrying on as before!

At a time when death was a constant threat, the friends detail their health. Lady Luxborough writes of a trembling hand, of an irregular pulse and of fevers that confine her to bed for weeks at a time. Her arthritis troubles her and she complains of the cold; of "paralytic fingers which will not obey the dictates of my heart" [31]. Shenstone, too, is subject to recurring fevers and is embarked upon a constant search for a purge to relieve his digestive problems. All of which helps to explain the anxiety caused when letters went astray, which they frequently did.

Many of the letters have numerous postscripts written at intervals throughout the day or several days. They are witty. Barrells' garden is a "ferme negligée"; and they illustrate how perceptive Henrietta is, as when the tone deaf Mr Outing parrots the opinion of others in expressing his enthusiasm for Handel's *Judas Maccabaeus*. "...if his ear is not good enough to distinguish the harmony, it serves to hear what the multitude say of it" [32] she points out. The language used is apt. Henrietta's description of life's "chequered chances" evokes the hand of fate. And autumn which, "...if it does not afford all the gaieties of Spring and Summer... is attended with fewer disappointments"[33], serves as a metaphor for life. Whether illustrating the discomfort of travel; "I don't love to jumble in a post chaise alone"[34], or contemplating her enjoyment of simple pleasures, she shows herself to be mistress of her craft.

Not everyone would agree. Horace Walpole branded her Ladyship's correspondence as "insipid" and without "wit", an indictment which has coloured the perception of generations of readers. He was unwilling to credit the freshness and spontaneity of the letters and, it would seem, did not understand what she was aiming to do. "I follow the rule I give and write what comes uppermost"[35] she explains, for she is conducting a conversation on paper.

Henrietta's letters provide excellent primary source material. From them we learn that it was not unusual for the host to thank the visitor for calling. Frequently guests would arrive in time for breakfast – and it was accepted practice for uninvited callers to ask if they might be shown around the garden. They illustrate her courage, chart her achievements – her sadness and joy. Most importantly, the letters provide a backdrop against which her aspirations can be measured.

Chapter 11

MY BROTHER BOLINGBROKE

Henrietta's letters are punctuated with references to her brother and such was his influence that it is not feasible to write about her without including him. It was after all, Bolingbroke who was responsible, together with her husband and other members of the St John family, for Mrs Knight's exile at Barrells – an exile which as the years passed he was to regard as less than fair. But by then the damage was done and the inclination to take further action not sufficiently strong. This is why Bolingbroke has a chapter to himself in which the puzzle of the man is revealed. For loved and admired by his sister, Harry Bolingbroke was in fact feared and detested by many, which is why the opening passage from Churton Collins' *Bolingbroke and Voltaire*, may be seen to provide a relevant starting point from which to proceed.

> *We have little respect for his public conduct; we have no liking for his personal character; we regard his political writings with suspicion and his metaphysical writing with contempt* [1].

This is a tempting view to take of Henrietta's adored eldest brother – her confidant and guide. A man who in his outrageous personal life was still to find time to nurture the genuine love that he bore his young sister. Whose political life was to witness his meteoric rise in the British Cabinet, matched by an equally rapid descent; a downfall which obliged him to flee the country to France for plotting with the Jacobins to restore the Old Pretender to the British throne as a Catholic James III.

It is a tempting view of the author of *Dissertations upon Parties* and *Idea of a Patriot King*, Bolingbroke titles which are said to have helped lay the foundation for "modern" Tory political thought – which were written upon his return to England when he was still hungry for political power – which are Machiavellian in the way they would seem to advocate expediency.

Especially it is a tempting view to take of the man who treated his first young wife, Frances Winchombe, so cruelly, depriving her of her property and inheritance. A man who was to describe his first marriage as "a trifling piece of news" and was repeatedly unfaithful. Indeed, it was not without cause that Jonathan Swift composed those wicked lines for a summerhouse at Bucklebury, their country estate, used for dubious pastimes:

From business and the noisy world retired
Nor vexed by love nor by ambition fired,
Gently I wait the call of Charon's boat
Still drinking like a fish and f... like a goat [2].

Frances died young – at the age of thirty-nine – and a description of her on her sick bed vividly portrays her suffering;

No one who saw her lying wasted on her bed and who remembered her beauty her
sweet ways and her unselfish life, could fail to be stirred [3].

This is the man who (presumably) kept hidden from his adoring younger sister the more squalid aspects of his private life. The man beloved and adored by his second wife, Marie Claire, the former Marquise de Villette – a lady who fared so much better than her predecessor and towards whom, it has to be said, he behaved admirably.

Bolingbroke was an enigma. A driven man – by vanity mostly – but in his dealings with these two women, the only women that he treated with any semblance of respect, he seems to have shown actual concern. Otherwise he was beguiling, manipulative and a sexual bully. He was physically attractive with an iron constitution and much charm; was super-charged, talented and when expedient, hardworking.

In those early days when Henrietta was a child, drinking and whoring took up much of Bolingbroke's time. As a young man his drunken revels in the East end of London would last for weeks at a time and it is no surprise that he contracted syphilis in his twenties, for his sexual adventures were preferably with street girls.

And a few years later, what is to be made of a man who became intimate with the Marquis de Guiscard, an erstwhile monk and sacrilegious libertine who poisoned one of his mistresses and was personally involved in the torture, by racking, of one of his own stewards he suspected of thieving?

Then there was bear-baiting at the Bear Garden in Hockley near Clerkenwell Green. There was cock fighting at the Cock Pit, dog fighting and bull baiting; cats let loose with fireworks attached to their tails to amuse the crowds. Bolingbroke with his "Dear Rake", alias Thomas Coke, later Lord Lovell of Leicester, were present at these events which, it can be noted, even in the eighteenth century were not approved by all. Certainly not by Alexander Pope, frequently a guest in later years at Dawley, Bolingbroke's country estate. In his polemic *Against Barbarity to Animals*, Pope writes of the cruelty that has become "almost a distinguishing character of the British Race". He continues:

> *We should find it hard to vindicate the destroying of anything that has life merely out of wantonness; yet in this principle our children are bred up, and one of the first pleasures we allow them, is the licence of inflicting pain upon poor animals* [4].

He denounces the "sports" of bull baiting and cock fighting. He fulminates against the torture of cats and owls, "who are a sort of feathered cats". And Pope is not alone, for a few years later we come across various members of Henrietta's Warwickshire Coterie voicing the same criticisms. "One should not destroy an insect" writes William Shenstone, "one should not quarrel with a dog without a reason sufficient to vindicate one through all the courts of morality" [5]. Richard Graves was concerned about the flogging of carriage horses and the skinning of live eels on the streets of London. Baffled by:

The unaccountable Disposition towards cruelty exercised against the Brute creation which is frequently observed among the general classes of Mankind who have not been restrained by natural sentiments or refined by a liberal education.

He supports his argument by quoting Ovid who singled out priests "the first Butchers or Sacrificers, (who) led the way to cruelty and slaughter" [6].

But to return to Bolingbroke. No such concerns were felt by him, a man unrestrained "by natural sentiment" and impervious to "the admonishments of a liberal education". Although he did write a good deal about "virtue" and "honour", toying with such concepts as a gamester with his dice. When young, he had posed as a man of letters and a patron of poets. To this end he had introduced himself to Dryden, inveigling himself into the great man's company. To good effect, for it can be seen that Dryden's translation of Virgil is prefixed by lines of Bolingbroke's own which at best are mediocre and which in any case are both patronising and ingratiating:

But Nature grown strongly kind
With all her fairest gifts adorned your mind
So Sultan like, in your Seraglio stand
While waiting Misses wait for your command;
Thus in decay, no want of rigour find
Such is your fancy, boundless is your mind [7].

What, one wonders, did Dryden feel about being described as "in decay"? At the time he would have been in his fifties and at the height of his creative powers – but no doubt blue blood and the possibility of patronage outweighed all else.

As for Henrietta? At this time she was yet to be born and the "age gap" between brother and sister may be one of the reasons why they were to become so close. Certainly, Bolingbroke's love for Henrietta was not self-seeking and although it can be argued that he betrayed her over her later problems with John Dalton, yet he never joined the chorus of her detractors except to express astonishment at her choice – "the worst poet in Christendom". He also attempted an unsuccessful reconciliation with Robert Knight, did his best to see that she remained financially secure. His letters to her are supportive and loving.

During his exile in France, Bolingbroke and Henrietta corresponded frequently. In her he perceived all the "symptoms of a good heart", rejoiced in the belief that she entertained "both sentiment and wit" and repeatedly assured her that "it is impossible to love you more better I do" [8]. He sent her presents to which she was quick to respond, and invited her confidences, especially during those periods of her marriage when she spent much time at La Planchette, and her role as hostess there was becoming extremely irksome. Then he was to assure her that "you write in confidence to me" while encouraging her to continue in her "duty":

> *You must go through it and do the honours of it, my dear girl, as well as you can.*
> *You owe that to Mr Knight, who must like what his father likes...* [9].

It was unpalatable advice but it was sweetened with welcome criticism of the old man's expensive life-style and the company he kept. Guests whose tastes were far removed from Henrietta's own.

After the breakdown of the Knights' marriage and his sister's exile to Barrells, it was her brother and not Henrietta's father, Lord St John, who was responsible for most of the negotiations. It was Bolingbroke who, with a prick of conscience assured her that "all I can do shall be done to mend the unfortunate circumstances in which your own family has helped to pin you down" [10]. A comment which comes very near to admission of Henrietta's innocence.

Later in 1742, it was Bolingbroke who came to his sister's aid when her father died and she came into her inheritance in the form of a £2000 bond. Earlier when her brother, Hollis, died she had been left a share, worth £17 per annum, in Covent Garden Theatre and also some family jewellery; but it was this latest "windfall" which was to prod her husband into action. He wrote to his wife of "the great change in your circumstances" before coming to the unacceptable (for Bolingbroke) conclusion that Henrietta was now sufficiently affluent to accept a twenty per cent reduction in her agreed marriage settlement. Mr Knight suggested that his wife's £500 a year be reduced to £407.

Four years earlier in 1738, Bolingbroke on Henrietta's behalf had accepted "the best advice of chancery lawyers", in an attempt to persuade her husband to become "somewhat more reasonable than now seems to be promised by his present disposition" [11]. Then as now the problem had been about money, and he was again to be involved in a legal battle with an intransigent brother-in-law who would seem to have grown more perverse, entrenched and obstinate as the years had passed. In the end Henrietta was not to lose her income, an outcome which suggests that when dealing with money, Henry Bolingbroke was on firmer ground than when involving himself with the "airy-fairy" stuff of human emotions, hurt feelings and wounded pride.

The year that Hollis died in 1738, was also the year that Bolingbroke was to sell Dawley, his red brick Queen Anne mansion which he had bought in 1728, and which figures prominently in this brother and sister story. The house was set in contrived and regimented gardens near Uxbridge in Middlesex but it was not this that caught Bolingbroke's eye so much as a cluster of disused farm buildings on the land. At this time it was fashionable for the wealthy to "play" at being farmers, a "game" which would enable Bolingbroke to put these to good use. It was not to be long before he began to think of his home as a "farm". He had his large entrance hall decorated with farming implements: rakes, hoes, spades and scythes all outlined in bold charcoal, imitating the décor of farmhouse kitchens of the time. His letters were soon to be headed "From my Farm" and he devoted his mornings to playing "farmer among his haycocks" presumably directing his labourers in their duties.

The estate at Dawley figures prominently in Henrietta's letters. References to "my brother's farm" and "before my brother sold his farm" abound. From her we learn that it was at Dawley that Bolingbroke entertained many of those glittering names that remain familiar, even today. Among them were Alexander Pope and John (Johney) Gay of *The*

Beggars Opera fame whose character, Macheath, satirising Robert Walpole as "Mac the knife", caused much merriment.

On these occasions we learn that guests would spend their afternoons in the orangery, a triumph of magnificent classicism far removed from the environs of a working farm. This was an elegant "taster" of what was to follow which was dinner served in a white panelled dining room on a shining mahogany table set with a profusion of silver and lit with candles to cast a warm glow. Here it was that conversation, lubricated with a superfluity of wine would have flowed.

As a young woman in the seventeen twenties Henrietta was a frequent guest at Dawley – one of the few women present except for Marie Claire, her brother's wife, and the very fashionable Duchess of Queensbury. Marie Claire, the possessor of a remarkable intellect and a woman of impeccable connections, had married Bolingbroke as soon as she decently could upon the death of his unfortunate first wife. Not only was she wealthy, she was also beautiful and was to prove herself equal to the (almost impossible) task of making and keeping her husband happy. The Duchess of Queensbury was beautiful too, but she was as renowned for her affectation of poverty. It pleased her – not to "play" at being a shepherdess as was popular at the time – but to dress as a peasant woman, on one occasion attending a ball at St James' Palace dressed in brown serge!

And what of Henrietta? At Dawley Bolingbroke's sister was a star in her own right. She was renowned for her conversation, her wit and vivacity. For her "Latin" looks, her luxuriant "crown" of dark hair and her good nature. She was a beauty – but one unspoiled by the compliments she was used to receiving. She was able to take her place among this group of super-charged and highly intellectual men with equanimity. Whatever turn the conversation took: literature perhaps? Or music, politics, philosophy or religion – she would contribute; but more importantly she would listen and learn from the exchanges across this dining table that were to provide a fitting education for the future literary hostess of Barrells Green. All of which calls to mind the question of whether such experiences would have helped to make Henrietta a suitable wife for a man like Robert Knight? A man of lesser clay – one who would have appeared at a disadvantage among these intellectual giants. Before her marriage, here is already a clue which points towards its eventual breakdown.

In sadder times Mrs Knight was to remember her visits to Dawley with happiness but also with regret for their passing. And it would have been with the same admixture of feeling that years later in 1747, and after over a decade at Barrells, she visited her brother and sister-in-law now settled at Battersea Manor, the family's ancestral home where they had been living since 1744. The old house was in an appalling state of repair as Marie Claire testifies:

> *When we build up on one wide it seems to fall down on the other, and the workmen never seem to finish, tho' we only do what is absolutely necessary to shelter us from the rain [12].*

By 1747, Bolingbroke was at a low ebb. He had managed to engineer a return to Britain; his bribes had eventually seen to that – hut there was no sign of a return to British politics and he was to remain in the political wilderness for the rest of his life. His letters to Lord Marchmont are filled with bitterness:

> *I see few of the people in this part of the world... than even you would imagine. Some who leaned upon me, such as I was, in their days of lameness, have laid me by as a useless implement, since the angel stirred the waters, and they got into the pool and were cured [13].*

and those to Henrietta infused with an unmitigated gloom that prompted her to act. She determined upon this visit in spite of the fact that, technically, she was breaking her commitment to keep away from the London area. In the event, Lord Luxborough either did not know or chose to do nothing about it, for it is likely that he would not have wanted another confrontation with his ailing brother-in-law. Especially if the rumours were true, and he was at this time fully occupied (with another lady).

So it was that brother and sister were to be together under the same roof for the first time in decades. Sitting in the warm summer sun beneath trees that fringed the river, they would have had many memories to share. Of Herriot's mama and King George's liking for her stewed apricots – of politics, and old friends and Court gossip. They would have reminisced of Dawley and its glittering coterie of visitors. Of Pope's villa near by at Twickenham with its spectacular "grotto", a "kind of open temple" with its shell walls lined inside with a myriad fragments of glass. A fairy place which, when the doors were closed, became in an instant "a Camera Obscura, on the walls of which all the objects of the river, hills woods boats are forming a moving picture" [14].

In the evening they would ensconce themselves, the three of them, in the one truly comfortable room of the house, that most beautiful "roome wainsitted with ceadar" where Bolingbroke had his desk and kept a number of his books; where the walls, panelled from floor to ceiling, would glow on colder evenings in the flickering firelight.

Henrietta's visit may be compared with the opening of a photograph album. The catalyst for a flood of dormant memories, it would have brought comfort and laughter as well as tears. Only with regret would her Ladyship have prepared to return to Barrells and the life of necessity she had succeeded in making her own. But return she did although it was not to be long before further bad news began to take its toll of her health. First she was to hear of the death of her brother, Jack St John, who had been so unsympathetic during her earlier troubles. Surprisingly she had always been fond of him and his demise was to trigger one of those "nervous feavours" to which she had always been prone.

It was also to cause problems back at Battersea where Bolingbroke decided to take upon himself the education of Jack's fourteen-year-old son, Frederic, now heir to the St John title. This proved to be a rash and disastrous move. The boy turned out to be morose and lazy and his behaviour to have a deleterious effect upon the already fragile health of Marie Claire. Indeed she was to become so alarmingly ill that Bolingbroke had no option but to remove his nephew from the house. He was sent abroad with a tutor to the University of Caen. That same winter, the Bolingbrokes moved house; from the draughty old manor to a much smaller and rented domicile in Soho where medical help was more readily summoned without the complication of the river. It was to be here that Marie Claire's husband devoted himself to her care in a manner so unlike his former self that one is left gasping.

In one of her last letters to her great friend Lady Denby, Bolingbroke's wife describes the regime:

> *My hermit and I go to bed before six o'clock. He gives himself up entirely to looking after me, in fact this is his only occupation.*

She concludes that she cannot express "how touched I am by his love and care" [15].

Marie Claire died on 18 March 1750, leaving her husband inconsolable. "My heart is broken, my spirit crushed and my body crippled. I am the most miserable of men" [16]. But in spite of his grief with which Henrietta could only empathise from afar, he was able to effect a moving tribute for his wife's memorial:

> *Born of a noble family*
> *Bred in the Court of Lewis 14, (sic)*
> *She reflected a lustre on the former*
> *By the superior accomplishments of her mind;*
> *She was an ornament to the latter*
> *By the amiable dignity and grace of her behaviour.*
> *She lived,*
> *The honour of her own sex*
> *The delight and admiration of ours.*
> *She dyed,*
> *An object of imitation to both,*
> *With all the firmness that religion*
> *Can inspire*
> *Aged 74 the 18 March*
> *1750* [17].

This one might imagine was the end – save it was not: for Marie Claire's daughter and her husband, the Marechal de Montmorin were soon to contest her mother's will on the grounds that her second marriage had never taken place. This was untrue, but as for some reason no marriage certificate was traced in France, their cause was given credence. Bolingbroke writes to Henrietta of his distress:

> *Montmorin is a strange example of ingratitude and injustice, and his suit is as strange an example of what Chicane can do against the plainest Right* [18].

He points out that he expects the proceedings to drag on "possibly to the end of my life" and adds that he can feel no tranquillity until they are over, or maybe never.

What concerned Bolingbroke was the memory of his dead wife whom he wished to be remembered as Viscountess Bolingbroke and not as his Mistress. There was also the question of money – there usually is! If Bolingbroke lost his lawsuit, he would lose a considerable income from Marie Claire's extensive estates, and the thought that her daughter might have some justifiable claim did not cross his mind. But in any case, now is not the time to reflect upon his affairs except to show how they were to affect Henrietta.

As one has come to expect, the news of her brother's distress was to make the tender hearted sister ill. She turned to her dear friend William Shenstone for comfort and her words show clearly who **she** believes to be in the right:

> *My own spirits are much lowered by my Brother Bolingbroke's misfortune; which thunderbolt fell upon him quite unexpectedly by the injustice or unskillfulness of French jurisprudence and the chicane of their lawyers* [19].

Meanwhile there was talk of Bolingbroke visiting Henrietta at Barrells – even of settling there. "My brother Bolingbroke" she writes excitedly:

is everyday in expectation to hear some account from France of his troublesome law-suit. After that, he will determine what to do. He seems inclined to end his days with me: if so, we will be a Hermit and Hermitess in reality... [20].

How welcome to Henrietta would such a turn of affairs have been. No longer the empty fireside after guests had left; no longer the worry of finding a suitable travelling companion when she set out in her coach for the Leasowes... But these were to prove "pipe dreams" for it was not to be. Whilst Bolingbroke waited anxiously at Battersea for news from France, his doctors discovered a cancerous growth on his face and forbade him to travel, an ultimatum which did little to lessen his enthusiasm for his sister's company. "I cannot tell you how much I was affected by your letter of the 12th" he writes, adding that instead of travelling to Barrells he is now making arrangements for Henrietta to visit him at Battersea;

If therefore you can come hither, the sooner you come the more comfort you will give me, and I will send a coach with a set of horses to meet you when and where you will appoint [21].

It seemed an excellent alternative and one with which her Ladyship was pathetically keen to comply. But she had again become ill of "a dangerous bilious feaver", no doubt triggered by worry and was unable to leave her bed. So as the clock ticked away the hours at Battersea and Barrells, both were to fix their hopes upon the following Saturday week when "My Brother Bolingbroke is to send a set of horses from Battersea... to fetch me to him" [22].

Henrietta's keenness to set out is reflected in her letters to Shenstone. She awaits her doctor's arrival "by my bedside". She repeats "my medicines every two hours, hoping to advance my cure" and touchingly asserts that surely "I must be dieing if I do not (go)" [23]. But in spite of all this her Ladyship did not go. She could not. Her fever lingered on and so did Bolingbroke, alone at Battersea. He died on 12 December 1751 and they never met again.

So ended an important chapter in Henrietta's life. With Bolingbroke's death she had lost a brother who concerned himself, if not always successfully, at least passionately with the welfare of his dearest sister. And after this, further troubles were to come upon her. Her daughter was to create a scandal, leave her husband and elope to France. Her oldest friend, Frances, now Duchess of Somerset was soon to die and she was to be left bereft with only Shenstone to turn to – a man whose many commitments were to make him less readily available.

Henrietta's grief at the death of her brother was extreme. But she was grieving for a man whose character she had not really known. For there were two Harry Bolingbrokes; the monster and the marvel and she had only known the latter. The one to whom she could always turn for advice and aid – not the one who cheated on his first wife – abused his trust and position. Not the man who made a god of expediency and enjoyed the "sports" of bear and bull baiting.

Such was the enigma of his brilliant but perverted mind. It is how things were, and one is forced to admit that Henrietta's life would have been poorer without his looming presence even though to many it must seem that his weaknesses outweighed his strengths.

Chapter 12

LITERARY INTERESTS

As has been seen, it was soon after his first invitation to Barrells in 1739, that Shenstone began to send Mrs Knight his verses. At first it was to impress a lady of quality but later, as he came to appreciate the acuteness of her perception, it was to seek advice. It was not to be long before a love of literature became the driving force of a friendship that was to mean much to them both. Before setting out for London in 1741, Shenstone wrote to Henrietta, enclosing his song, *When Bright Ophelia Treads the Green*. Anxious for a favourable response he stipulates how welcome a letter from her would be:

> *If I were to receive a letter from you as I put my foot into the stirrup, I bid Mrs Arnold take in her Bottle, for I had no occasion for Cordial* [1].

The pleasure of a letter from Mrs Knight would outweigh even the delights of his housekeeper's fruit juice – what flattery!

And it had the desired effect. Delighted with the compliment, Henrietta responded at once to demonstrate how "greatly obliged" she is for verses which have "already given much pleasure and will do so as often as I read (them)" [2]. So it was that the poems continued. Upon his return home, Mrs Knight becomes Shenstone's "Queen of the May", his "Fair Asteria" in whose company even the rigours of winter lose their bite. In the meantime Henrietta reads his poems "eagerly", pronounces them "extremely pretty and very poetical", and provides the young man with a much needed boost to his morale.

Before long Shenstone was to send Mrs Knight his *Verses to a Lady of Quality,* and later his *The Dying Kid* which contains those delightful lines redolent for us, today, of Walt Disney:

...of what delight he stood
To trace his features in the flood
Then skipped aloof with quaint amaze
And then drew near again to gaze [3].

The poem warns of the little creature's impending death when he will be culled to prevent him in his maturity from inflicting harm. Henrietta's response implies her willingness to see the situation from Shenstone's point of view:

Your Kid moves compassion; but it is a comfort to think (as you observe) how many evils it would have done, if it had lived to be old... [4].

But this was not always the case. Shenstone's inscription, *O You That Bathe in Courtly Blysse,* is a poem which contrasts those who "Toyle in Fortune's giddy sphere", with others, like the poet and his friends, content with simple, rural pleasures. The poem had been "posted" on the back of Shenstone's newly completed "Gothick" alcove and was much admired by his neighbour, Mr Lyttelton, who had brought his friends, Mr Pitt (the future Prime Minister) and Mr Miller along to view the Leasowes. But there was one couplet which they did not like and which now completes the final stanza:

Nor yet deride the beechen bowle
In which he quaffs the limpid springs [5].

These were the same lines maintained by Henrietta to be "Vastly pretty (but) in some other place" [6]; a pastoral image unsuitable for a "Gothick" seat and alcove. She may have been right. She certainly was in her comments relating to Shenstone's *In Cool Grot* (see Chapter 9), suggesting "mossy cell" (in line one) to be preferable to "fringed cell" – and "ill betide" in the final couplet to "harm betide". It is of interest today to see that the poet accepted the former but not the latter alteration.

It was around this time that we first learn of Henrietta's own poetry (which gets a chapter to itself) and which she sent, as did all the Coterie, on its round for friendly comment. As we shall see, Shenstone read much of it with approbation and was instrumental in encouraging her to persevere. Meanwhile the exchanges continued with her Ladyship, including the poet's *Ballad of Queen Elizabeth* in a "packet" to the Duchess of Hertford, and Shenstone supplying Henrietta with his *Ballad of Jemmy Dawson*, a dirge about the execution of a young man as a traitor.

Then there were Shenstone's *Elegies,* poems that he had dangled before her Ladyship for many months before she was eventually to get to see them – a privilege for which she had to work hard. They were first mentioned in June 1748. "I have written a large collection of Elegies on almost every melancholy subject that I could recollect" [7], he tells her. But it was not until the following November that the poet again postulates "some very solemn Elegies which I shall shortly put into your hands" [8]. Nothing happened. The weeks marched on and Henrietta was obliged to resort to plain talking in order to obtain a glimpse of the elusive manuscripts which by now had been collected in the poet's "Green Book".

"I am impatient for the Green Book" [9] she reminds him, and a week later, "the Green Book will add greatly to my pleasure" [10]. Finally, on 12 December 1748, in a last attempt to prize his poems from him, Lady Luxborough was to begin her letter with an image of Shenstone at work:

Methinks I see you by your chimney piece, your pen in your hand and the... Green Book before you, just going to express with poetical elegance some refined or sublime thought... [11].

It was a device that worked! Shenstone parted with his precious manuscripts – but not before begging his friend "to make some kind of mark on such as you should least dislike" [12].

At last Henrietta was able to deliver her verdict. She liked the poetry – which she assures him "will please better judges as they do me". But not the preface to them which she finds over long and wordy, and likely to make readers "...lay down the book before they got to what (it) is mean't to introduce them to!" [13]. A valid point even if a little inelegantly expressed.

In fact, Shenstone had had problems with his preface – at one time even considered dispensing with it altogether. So what Henrietta had to say caused little surprise and encouraged him to return to his re-writing and to salvage one glorious phrase in which he describes the ultimate elegiac style to be "flowing as a mourner's veil" [14].

Later her Ladyship was to encourage the downhearted poet with his poem, *Rural Elegance*. The verses are in praise of Percy Lodge, the country retreat of the Duchess of Somerset and when he was requested not to publish her name, he had taken this to mean that she objected to the entire project. He stopped work and for many months throughout 1753, Henrietta undertook the difficult task of persuading him otherwise. "...finish the Ode you must", she tells him in January of the same year, and in December after months of pressure:

> *Had our Duchess not intended you should publish it, what need had she of stars or dashes instead of her and of her habitation's names? Do not deprive Her Grace of the compliment you intended her...* [15].

Ultimately she was to prevail, the Duchess was delighted and due to Henrietta the public was not deprived of one of the most delightful of Shenstone's odes.

In 1752, Henrietta copied the poet's *Ode to Indolence*, which she tells him "pleases me much" and she was also very involved in the re-casting of another of Shenstone's well-known and well-loved poems – his *A Pastoral Ballad*. He had been having trouble with Canto III, *Solicitude*. "Never", he writes to Henrietta in 1755, "was I puzzled more than in tricking out that Pastoral Fop, Sir Paridel". And he continues in a way that makes the modern reader smile:

> *Your Ladyship, if you cannot... approve,... will I'm sure assist a poor bewilder'd Poet who applies to you as a Genius, a Florist and a Friend* [16].

The final version of Canto III was the fruit of much re-casting as the poem went back and forth between the Leasowes, Barrells and Graves' Rectory in Somerset; until the clock stopped and Dodsley who was to publish it in Volume IV of his *Miscellanies,* declared that he could wait no longer. Which turned out not to matter, for the poem was well received.

It was to this same Volume IV that Shenstone, in his capacity as co-editor, submitted four of Henrietta's poems, and to two of them, "tryfling Songs which dropt from my pen" [17], he decided to make minor adjustments. He was to wish he had not! For disapproval from Barrells was such that the poet was obliged to extricate himself by means of a grovelling apology. Because she writes her "lively pieces almost extempore", because "an expression not altogether exact" might have escaped her attention; "I am therefore most humbly to crave your Ladyship's pardon for proposing what I thought might be some improvement to your verses..." [18].

One wonders what on earth Henrietta could have said? As the letter has not survived we can only surmise; but it would seem that the poems were not such "tryfling Songs" after all. And the spat, if that is what it was, did not last long for her Ladyship was soon wishing Shenstone's future path to "be strewn with petals", presumably to ease his way. Even so the incident is of interest because it shows that in keeping with the rest of her class, Henrietta, on occasion, could be haughty. She could be generous and loving as we know – but in common with the rest of us she had her weaknesses too.

Discussing poetry, and the writing of it, as a following chapter will show, provided Henrietta with an abiding interest. She and Shenstone spent many happy fireside hours reading aloud – from plays and novels as well as poems and this together with her interest in her garden, provided her with the intellectual muscle and discipline of purpose so essential to her well being.

Chapter 13

HENRIETTA'S POETRY

As did many young women of the time, Henrietta wrote poems. These, like her letters, have been dismissed as inconsequential; a mistaken view, not least because when taken in context, the verses provide us with a clearer understanding of her situation at Barrells. They also illumine her friendship with Shenstone and the turbulence of her inner emotional life.

It has been seen how in those early days at Marlborough, Henrietta's friendship with Frances and the poet, Elizabeth Rowe, was instrumental in consolidating her enjoyment of poetry – and how during that time they all, including John Dalton, wrote rhyming letters to each other which were responsible for a good deal of fun. Now it is necessary to take another look at lines from one of those early communications penned by Mrs Knight to Dalton in 1734, when she was unwell and unable to accompany the Hertfords into the country:

No sooner was Adonis fled
To breathe parnassian air,
But I with sorrow dropp'd my head
And tore my platted hair [1].

There is a good deal of interest here, for the verse suggests more than a passing acquaintance with *Hamlet* and the First Player's parody of Aeneas' *Tale to Dido,* a moment in which Shakespeare is also enjoying himself:

But who – ah woe! – had seen the mobbled queen
...a clout upon her head
Where late the diadem stood, and for a robe
...a blanket in the alarm of fear caught up [2].

There are numerous other linguistic similarities throughout Henrietta's poem of which one more will suffice. For example, her lines:

Deserted Paphos now appears
The set of silent woe,

mirror the First Player's description of the empty city:

A silence in the heavens –
A bold wind speechless, and the orb below
As hush as death...

None of this is to be taken too seriously – but the point is made to demonstrate that Mrs Knight had the education, the humour – she was clearly **happy** at this time – and the facility to amuse herself in this way. The lines capture her mood just as her later poetry reflects her unhappiness at Barrells.

It was not until she arrived at Barrells that Henrietta began to pen more thoughtful verse. Then with Shenstone's encouragement, she was to produce work which, even if not to be classed as literature, is pleasing to the ear and has something to say. That many of her poems have not survived is unfortunate. Verses to her secretary, *Lines to Mr Outing*, have not, which is a pity because it was a poem much admired by her circle of friends. However the poems that we do have are of interest for their recurring themes of loneliness and imprisonment; ideas which her letters frequently translate into insistent invitations to visit and protestations that travel is difficult without a companion; which it was, and is why Mr Outing was frequently pressed into service.

In her poems the themes are more explicit. *Written to a Near Neighbour in a Tempestuous Night*[3] tells of her feelings of isolation after Shenstone has left:

But now alone, by storms opprest
Which harshly in my ears resound.

Henrietta always dreaded the time when her guests were obliged to leave – for it was then that she felt at her most vulnerable, especially on a stormy night which prevented her from sleeping and there was:

No cheerful voice with witty jest
No jocund pipe to still the sound.

Another of the poems, *Written in Winter*[4], returns to this concept of loneliness. Described by Shenstone as "equal to any song in the language", a comment which, if over generous, at least points its merit, the verses describe against a backdrop of winter chill, the isolation felt when a loved one is absent. Both Henrietta and Shenstone dreaded the approach of winter, for then the roads were frequently impassable and visiting impossible. This was a time of year when "country puts" as her Ladyship charmingly described country dwellers, were obliged to settle by a lonely fireside.

Written in Winter demonstrates an interesting similarity with Shenstone's poem, *The Landscape*[5]. Although Henrietta describes a winter scene:

The hills all white with snow
Leave me dejected and forlorn!

and Shenstone's poem is evocative of summer-time:

Was ever scene so deck'd with flowers?
Were ever flowers so gay?

the concern of them both is with the separation of lovers – and her Ladyship's lines:

The frozen brooks and pathless vales
Disjoin my love and me:

Can be seen to echo Shenstone's:

That verdant hill and silver stream
Divides my love and me.

Here it is tempting to translate Henrietta's conventional use of "Damon" throughout her poem into "Shenstone". When she is left alone, what pleasure is to be found in:

...birds or brooks
Or any joy that's near?

A predicament that is made plain in the last two lines of the second stanza:

Heavy the lute and dull the books
While Damon is not here.

Her Ladyship and William Shenstone enjoyed a close friendship – one that suited them both. Two lonely people neither of whom, either wanted or were able to undertake the commitment of marriage. Henrietta because, technically, she was still married and on her guard against any further hint of scandal; and the latter because whatever her Ladyship's situation, he would seem to have been incapable of making up his mind. But this did not prevent either of them from flirting with the idea of falling in love and the use that both make of the traditional Damons, Phylises and Flavias of the day, can be seen as a means of perpetuating this.

And even if it was the **idea** rather than love itself that attracted, there is no doubt that their relationship involved, by means of their shared interests – a marriage at any rate of minds. Both shared a passion for gardening. It was after all, in large part with Shenstone's help that Henrietta had re-fashioned her own garden at Barrells – and she well understood his aim to work with Nature to create a "modern" natural looking garden: one that meandered rather than marched, demonstrating a fluidity of line quite unlike the regimented symmetry of earlier seventeenth century estates. In her *Lines Written at a Ferme Ornée* [6] she makes this clear:

> *Where modest art in silence lurks conceal'd*
> *While Nature shines so gracefully reveal'd.*

Finally, with its theme of imprisonment, there is her Ladyship's *The Bullfinch in Town* [7], an "extremely elegant" poem with a poignancy, structure and choice of language that, arguably, lifts it into the realms of literature. It is a poem which may be seen as a metaphor for her Ladyship's exile at Barrells. She, as the bird in the title, is a "hapless captive" in a "...well-gilt cage remote from air". Like the hapless bullfinch with his "faded plumes", her health too, has suffered and his "one dull tune" replicates her own dullness from want of intellectual stimulation. When on occasion as she writes to Shenstone, she "might well have been a mole and lived underground" [8].

Henrietta's poem contrasts the lot of this captive bird whose imprisonment like her own, is "dearly bought", with the freedom of blackbirds "in fields where birds unfettered soar". The verses end with an image of her Ladyship outside in the meadows, attendant upon "the inviting spring". It is a joyful finale and one which illustrates how, in spite of her troubles, Henrietta has been determined to overcome them. Her Ladyship's poems are rich in imagery, from the "opera pinions" of the unfortunate bullfinch to the "treacherous wildfire" of the poet's overheated brain in *To a Near Neighbour in a Tempestuous Night*.

Submitted by Shenstone, four of the five verses discussed here were included by the publisher, Robert Dodsley in the Fourth Volume of his popular Miscellanies: *A Collection of Poems by Several Hands,* described by Byron as "the best thing of its kind".

A comment by the publisher concerning the contents of Volume IV, makes a fitting ending to any discussion of Henrietta's poetry. The Collection, he maintained, may not have included "castles and palaces", but it did entertain some "very pretty cottages". It is an opinion that would have pleased her Ladyship. For that is what her poems represent – "some very pretty cottages".

Chapter 14

HENRIETTA'S VISIT TO BATH

After her brother's death Henrietta had somehow dragged herself to London where she had stayed a while with her daughter and son-in-law. But the visit did little to improve her well-being and upon returning home to Barrells she turned for advice and treatment to Mr Holyoake. It was clear that she needed company to stop her brooding. It was felt that a change of air in an atmosphere conducive to physical and mental improvement was necessary so Mr Holyoake suggested Bath.

Bath was a town with many pleasant memories for Henrietta and although she was at first reluctant and viewed the long journey with trepidation, she finally accepted the advice that her doctor gave and embarked upon preparations for the visit. On 25 January 1752 she at last set off – in her "coach with a coronet" that had so impressed Shenstone. She took with her the faithful Joe and the reliable Mr Price who would take turns to drive the (four) horses; and in an age when "quality" was denoted by the opulence of the carriage and the livery of the servants, it is likely that the men would have been dressed for the part: would have worn gold braided narrow brimmed hats, leather breeches topped with a colourful jacket and linen shirt. All of which would have been an expensive undertaking.

Henrietta arrived in Bath during January after a journey which had taken two days. On the way down she broke her journey with a night at the New Inn in Gloucester which offered well-aired beds and a warming pan in every room to prove it. In the privacy of her own chamber she would have eaten her meal – not for a lady of her standing was the communal table supplied to stage coach passengers of the type that we meet in

Fielding's *Joseph Andrews*. Neither would she have wished to sample the fare provided by a company of strolling players who performed in a large back room. She would enjoy her fill of theatre, later, in Bath.

Her venue in Bath was the Orange Grove where she stayed with Mrs Hodgkinson highly recommended by Shenstone. Upon arrival the abbey bells pealed a welcome as they did for all "important" visitors and Henrietta was certainly that – even getting a mention in *The Bath Journal* which recorded "Arrived here Lady Luxborough" on 27 January 1752.

Not long after settling into her own suite of rooms and eating her first meal (dinner at four o'clock), her Ladyship, as was the custom, received a visit from Beau Nash – a gentleman she much admired. This was a "welcome" visit, or the "visit of ceremony of first coming", as it was known; one of the *Eleven Rules to be observed at Bath*, devised by the man, himself, and hung in elegant Gothic script upon the wall of the Pump Room. These included other imperatives such as:

- *That ladies coming to the Ball appoint a time for their footmen coming to wait on them home, to prevent disturbances and inconveniences to others.*

- *That gentlemen crowding before ladies at the Ball, show ill manners; and that none do so in the future – except such as respect nobody but themselves.*

- *That all whisperers of lies and scandal be taken as their author's* [1].

As can be seen, all were concerned with good manners, an ideal upon which the smooth running of Bath society and events depended. That Nash was overwhelmingly successful and that all did run as smoothly as planned, is attested for by Henrietta with enthusiasm. The aim of Beau Nash, she tells Shenstone, is:

> *To promote society, good manners, and a coalition of parties and ranks; to suppress scandal and late hours, are his views; and he succeeds rather better than his brother–monarchs generally do* [2].

He is, she says:

> *Our lawgiver... whose white hat commands more respect and non-resistance than the crowns of some kings, though now worn on a head that is in the eightieth year of its age* [3].

Perhaps we could do with a Beau Nash today, one cannot help feeling!

After a night's sleep, undisturbed one would hope by the peeling of the abbey bells and the voice of the "regular watch" which intoned each hour, Henrietta's next visitors were her two doctors, William Oliver and Jeremiah Peirce. Men whose very names inspire confidence and who "give me hopes" she reports to Shenstone, "that bathing and pumping will soon restore me the use of my hands" [4]. And so the experience began. What was it like?

A visit to Bath was a pleasing mix of medical imperatives and social delights. The medical routine was strict and consisted of daily visits to the King's Bath. There, at eight every morning, patients were conveyed by "friendly chairmen": either like oven ready chickens – wrapped in a blanket inside "a little black box the size of a coffin" [5]; or if this did not appeal, bathers could avail themselves of changing rooms provided near by. In fact people entered the water fully dressed. The men wore long linen drawers and matching jackets. The ladies wore ankle length skirts and linen jackets; were not considered to be suitably attired without a little pill box hat and a floating tray which would seem to have fulfilled the same kind of purpose as a modern day handbag.

Then they were ready to enter the baths – that "great smoking kettle" – in which every type of patient, suffering from all manner of diseases, immersed themselves. Here, bobbing up and down until obliged to make way for newcomers, were men and women of all ages, station and background – relaxed, weightless and hugger-mugger in conditions that were far from savoury. It was an experience later to be reinforced by a visit to the Pump Room where patients would queue between eight o'clock and ten to drink the waters. Now was the time for new friendships to be kindled and old acquaintances renewed. A time when patients who had braved bathing and were now pumping, could if they wished, look down upon newcomers who comprised the motley company of bathers below. And meanwhile because:

> *Music is wholesome, the doctors think,*
> *For ladies that bathe and for ladies that drink,* [6]

an orchestra provided by Nash and financed by public subscription, played suitable pieces by Purcell, Corelli or Arne's setting for *Where the Bee Sucks*, to entertain the guests.

After all this and having attended to the body, it was time to think of the soul; so most guests attended prayers in the abbey at eleven o'clock. Here another musical feast was in store and Henrietta would have heard Thomas Chilcot, the celebrated abbey organist, perform some of his own works in the style of Handel.

Afterwards the guests would have had time to enjoy the many social delights in which they were encouraged – expected even – to participate. High on the list were the booksellers, especially Fredericks where Henrietta paid her subscription of five shillings for the season which enabled her to make use of the library facilities that were offered. Then there was Mr Leake's Bookshop at number five, The Walks. Mr Leake was what today would be described as a "character" – "the Prince of all coxcombical Fraternity of Booksellers". A man who, continues Lord Orrery, "not having any learning himself... seems resolved to sell it as dear as possible to others" [7].

It was at Mr Leake's that Henrietta spent much time in the company of well-known local personages such as Ralph Allen of Prior Park and Richard Graves, an erstwhile member of her "Coterie" and now the popular Rector of Claverton. Here as well, would come many of the guests whom she had met at the Pump Rooms – to read pamphlets and newspapers and browse among the crowded shelves. There was an added attraction, too. For Mr Leake was the brother-in-law of the novelist, Samuel Richardson, whose novel, *Pamela*, written in the form of a series of letters, had propelled him to fame in 1740. It was a novel that both Henrietta and Shenstone had read – the latter pronouncing it "too prolix" and even suggesting suitable cuts! But none of this detracts from its general popularity at the time. Richardson's *Clarissa,* which followed soon after was to prove equally popular and lucky visitors to the shop were likely to meet the novelist in his plum coloured waistcoat and yellow wig which would have made him easily recognisable as he sat reading.

Beyond doubt, Leake's was the focal point of social life in Bath: the place to go and be seen. But what of the man himself? Leake, like all successful businessmen of his time, was assiduous in his observation of rank and looked "upon every Man distinguished by any Title, not only as his Friend, but his Companion, and treats him accordingly" [8]. Which was all very well, but the consequences for some were less pleasant as it meant that he would not deign to speak to a "Marquise whilst a Duke (was) in the Room...". Even so, he seems to have had time for Lady Luxborough who bought a number of books and pamphlets from him including: *The Lady's Companion* and, for two shillings, Dr Oliver's *Practical Essay on the Use and Abuse of Warm Bathing in Gouty Cases.*

As well as booksellers there were other equally popular attractions. Pastry cooks like Mr Gill, a man whose "creations" were so delicious that Christopher Anstey (who had written a series of verse letters concerning the adventures, in Bath, of a family called Blunderhead) was moved to write an amusing and mouth watering little poem in honour of them:

> *Of all the cooks the World can boast*
> *However great their skill,*
> *To bake, or fry, to boil, or roast,*
> *There's none like Master Gill.*

And in the final stanza readers are exhorted:

> *When e're ye droop, O taste the soup*
> *That's made by Master Gill* [9].

Then there were the linen drapers who sold "the newest and genteelist Patterns"; the milliners and the "toyshops" famous for their antique coins, standishes and seals. It was from one of these, that in an attempt to lift his spirits, Henrietta was to buy for Shenstone "a succession of elegant presents"; the same which Joe was to deliver "with great Care and Expedition".

Other attractions were the universally popular dances. On 3rd March in celebration of the King's birthday a special Ball, organised by Beau Nash and proclaimed by the firing of cannon, took place at Mr Simpson's Rooms. It was one of the few occasions at which her Ladyship put in an appearance and one of the reasons for this was the rigorous procedures always adopted at such times. First there was timing. All balls began at six and ended at eleven. Then there was the etiquette to which everyone rigorously adhered. Proceedings began with a minuet danced by the "two persons of highest distinction present". When this was over the lady then returned to her seat while the gentleman remained to await a new partner chosen for him by the Master of Ceremonies. Every succeeding couple was then obliged to follow the same routine, the gentleman always dancing with two ladies in succession. Gradually everybody joined in until the floor was crowded, after which the proceedings continued for a further two hours. Then at eight o'clock it was time for the country dances to get under way – until nine – when there was a much needed short break for tea and cakes. After this the dancing continued until eleven o'clock when Beau Nash brought the proceedings to an end. By lifting his finger he would bring the music to a halt and signal that ladies were to be handed to their chairs, indicating that the evening's revelry was over and all were homeward bound.

One may smile at the military precision with which these functions operated. But there can be no doubt that Nash's triumph of organisation achieved its desired effect. Discipline was maintained, interest held and every lady present had the benefit of a partner. "Wallflowers" were not left to linger.

In her letters to Shenstone, Henrietta makes little comment about balls such as this one, card playing or tea drinking which all went on in abundance. The reason is that the poet disliked all these things, but adored another of the entertainments which Bath had to offer – its theatre – and consequently her Ladyship has much more to say about this. She gives glowing accounts of a number of the theatrical experiences that the city has to offer. A place where:

> *Duchesses trudge the streets unattended (and) we also have friendly Othellos, Falstaffs, Richards the Third, and Harlequins who entertain one daily for half the price of your Garricks, Barrys, and Rich's...* [10].

"Bid business avaunt" she admonishes the poet who, at a low ebb, has excused himself on this account. And in a final bid to tempt him to come to Bath "...we can offer you friendly solitude, for one may be an Anchoret here without being disturbed by the question 'why?'" [11].

In the meantime she paid a visit to the new Orchard Street Theatre which had recently opened with "a good company of Performers, new Cloaths, Scenes etc" [12]. Here at the end of February she was to see Mr Bland in the title role of *Othello*, an experience partially spoiled by the heat and the over crowding. She also attended a performance of *Romeo and Juliet* at a rival establishment, Brown's Theatre, where performances were given in a play room situated under the ballroom at Mr Simpson's. This company was frequently patronised by Beau Nash and consequently had a large following among the nobility and gentry. Unaffected by the heat from an abundance of tallow candles which had ruined the earlier performance, Henrietta, on this occasion, enjoyed her evening – felt much more at home and writes enthusiastically of the experience.

Her Ladyship also went visiting. She accepted an invitation to see the Graves at Claverton Rectory and faithfully reported to Shenstone all that happened. She writes of "your friend... who does not leave his wife an inch" [13]. Was charmed by Lucy, the twenty-year-old mother of two who now entertained her Ladyship upon a favourite topic – gardening, offering her a polyanthus root when the time was ripe. Together they all walked, taking their time, round the large rectory garden and Graves presented her with a cornel tree. He also amused Henrietta with a verse upon his own brand of "natural" landscaping:

Hold! Hold good Joe, your sacrilegious hand
My taste I find you do not understand.
Root up that apple tree and plum.
The fruit they bear's no bigger than my thumb.
Yet fruit or flowers I count as useless dross,
But spare my real treasure, spare my moss [14].

Another visit was to Ralph Allen of Prior Park. Allen was to Bath what Matthew Boulton was to Birmingham – a philanthropist who contributed much to the city and who regularly entertained a coterie of intellectuals and professional men. It was here that Henrietta met Sarah Fielding in whose dark vivacity she might well have seen a mirror image of herself. Sister to a more famous brother, Henry Fielding, Sarah was also a novelist and at this time was in the middle of her three-volume novel, *David Simple*, a cautionary tale about a young man who sets out to find a friend uncorrupted by deceit or greed. A topical theme for today one might feel. Another guest was Lady Huntingdon whose extreme brand of Methodism encouraged her to approach Henrietta about the state of her "never dieing soul". She suggested that more time should be spent in religious contemplation and less upon social activities! But was forced to admit that her Ladyship's good humour and good nature (in the face of what one imagines must have seemed like provocative religious militancy) were very attractive traits. The world of patronage to which writers aspired and the rich and famous belonged was relatively intimate and there is an interesting link here with Henrietta's brother Bolingbroke. He and Marie Claire were both friendly with Lord Huntingdon, although the latter's wife would surely have made a most unlikely addition to the quartet.

On this occasion Henrietta also again met Samuel Richardson, a man whose rapid rise to literary fame had done little to alter his benign good humour, and the painter, William Hoare, who invited her to his studio to view his canvases. It was exhilarating – one invitation soon led to another and her Ladyship was to blossom in a whirl of social activity that encouraged her to forget her grief and her loneliness back at home.

But alas, the days passed too quickly and Henrietta's three month stay was soon at an end. It was time to return to Barrells. Soon her luggage was packed, her coach prepared, polished and inspected and her horses brought round from Stall Street. Then there were the good-byes and all the servants she had got to know tipped the expected guinea each – a considerable sum and one that her Ladyship could ill afford. All this before Henrietta, with Joe and Mr Price, was off with a store of stories to tell.

The journey home, which again took two days, was uneventful – or nearly so. Outside Cirencester they passed a dead highwayman swinging fully dressed in his wig and riding boots from a gibbet! Surely a reminder of the lurking dangers of the open road and the need for armed protection. Her Ladyship arrived in Warwickshire rejuvenated; but whether this was due to the "bathing and pumping" or simply that she had been away from the damp and cold of Barrells, it is not possible to say. At any rate she was now ready to enjoy again her life at home – thanks to her restored health and vigour.

Chapter 15

THE RETURN HOME

Back at Barrells, it did not take long for Henrietta to get down to doing what she most enjoyed. Revitalized, she tackled her correspondence with a new zest, entertained as frequently as she was able and continued to implement improvements to her home and gardens.

After journeying to Oxford on business, her home since April had been filled with company and by mid-July she was proud to be presiding over "eight people at table", a party which included her relation, Sir Peter Soames, and his son. At around this time she has sent away her post-chaise "to have new wheels put to it" [1], and the impression is that – briefly – the burden of life has been replaced with pleasure.

Outside she is still busy "making small improvements... in my Coppice", and along the pathway to it has planted a hedge which she hopes "will grow as quick as yours did" [2], she tells Shenstone. And it was not to be long before that same summer she visited the Leasowes to be met with "a very obliging, hospitable and pleasing reception" [3]. To her delight, a return visit within a matter of weeks was again to provide the pleasure of Shenstone's company at Barrells, where the occasion, "agreeable, though too short", passed quickly.

Neither was Henrietta idle indoors. She has decorated her bedroom and dressing room, filled in cracks in their respective ceilings so that they look "just as I would and as I believe you (Shenstone) would have it" [4]. When at her writing desk she was frequently interrupted by Mr John Reynolds, or Mr Bradley or Lady Plymouth's servant or any one of her numerous and delightful country parsons – which was just as she liked it, for her Ladyship was a social animal.

Planning visits and writing letters kept her busy. She was delighted by Sir George Lyttelton's approval of one of her poems – was making plans for future visits to the Plymouths, the Bradleys or Mrs Davis at Stratford. Life, for Henrietta, was good. Storm clouds had made way for sunshine but it was not to be long before the climate again would change.

Of course there were still some happy times ahead. A visit to the Leasowes in September 1754, when she was to admire improvements to the poet's "Walks and Cascades (which) make your place a Paradise in miniature" [5]. But by then she was complaining of "the weakness of my limbs which prevented my trampouzing as much as I used" [6].

For the truth is that Henrietta's health had again begun to deteriorate – a circumstance undoubtedly precipitated by her daughter's elopement in the February of the previous year with Sir Joshua Childs. It was at a time when her Ladyship was already depressed by the enforced loneliness of long winter evenings and now, "by the storm... of my Daughter's imprudence (to call it by no worse a name)... raised not only in her family, but in the World" [7], was to be brought by degrees to an extremely low ebb.

It was an event which both scandalized and titillated London society as is clear from a letter to Shenstone by his friend, John Scott Hylton. At the time the latter was staying in the capital and relates what had been going on with the gusto of a lip-smacking voyeur:

> *I can furnish you with few particulars of Mrs W...'s Amour. All I know is, her husband and other People had ocular Demonstration of her Guilt, by a servant Boy's boring three holes in the wainscot, which afterwards cut into one* [8].

One can imagine what memories such an incident would have stirred within Henrietta's heart and mind. Of John Dalton and her own "indiscretions", of her anger, misery and exile. Then there would have been concern about her daughter's uncertain future and it is not surprising that a resultant spell in bed was quickly the outcome. "I have never been below stairs since I wrote to you last (a month ago)" she tells Shenstone: and she complains of "a violent pain in my face and teeth (of) so bad a pen, so bad a head, so bad spirits..." [9].

Over the following months and years the list carries on and failing health was to make Henrietta ever more reliant upon her neighbours and friends. Now she admits to Shenstone that her "brightness... is only borrowed as that of the moon"; that when she is deprived of his company she "remain(s) a dull inanimate lump" [10]. Small things distress her as when letters do not arrive as regularly as she would like and her requests for visits became more demanding. Although she "had rather now deck a rural bower than Glitter on a birth night at court", yet she is obliged to admit that "the loss of neighbours and of limbs, make these bowers more irksome than inviting" [11].

During the seventeen fifties her dependence upon Shenstone grew. At the very time his horizons were expanding – hers contracted. When his advice as a man of letters, as editor and as landscape gardener, was sought by many, Henrietta, like an unpartnered girl at a ball, must wait on the sidelines for visitors or letters to arrive. It is a long time since the poet, a decade ago, had written for his "Queen of the May" that lovely little song, *Perhaps it is not Love* [12], a poem in which the line of the title becomes:

It is – it is love's subtle fire,
And under friendship lurks desire.

A poem which tells her of his failure to persuade himself otherwise.

Now she was older and ill. Her brother Bolingbroke was dead as was Parson Allen; and in 1754 her dear friend Frances, now Duchess of Somerset, was also to die. Henrietta's distress as one by one these links with her past were broken, taxed her already fragile health and precipitated the countdown to her final illness.

On several occasions, as in the summer of 1755, her Ladyship was to be disappointed when hopes of a visit from Shenstone were dashed. Although "Mrs Nugent visits me again (and) I go tomorrow to dine with a clergyman who seems to have some taste" [13], these calls were no substitute for what she really wanted: "...your (Shenstone's) company and Mr Hilton's in my shrubbery, my hermitage, my library and, in the evening at my fireside" [14].

Later that summer, her Ladyship was to suffer a further, cruel disappointment. Shenstone, a reluctant host, "apprehensive that I shall be ill or not at leisure to receive" [15], whatever that might mean, was entertaining Richard and Lucy Graves. They were all invited to Barrells but at the last moment the poet changed his mind and Richard and Lucy Graves turned up alone. That they arrived "without you" she lets Shenstone know, left her "disagreeably disappointed" which is an under statement for in fact she was extremely hurt. That Shenstone at this time was still preoccupied to the point of obsession with his nephew, young Dolman, and their ongoing legal battle, was no excuse.

In Henrietta's own words, she had once again been "dealt an unlucky hand as the gamesters say" and as always, the incident was to trigger a series of health problems which did little to improve her emotional well-being and much to lower her resistance to infection.

Her Ladyship's final illness began the following year, in February 1756, when she developed a severe cold, sore throat and hoarseness. It was to show no signs of clearing up and by the time she had been ill nearly a month, her Chaplain, Mr Holyoake, was sufficiently concerned to advise her to receive the last sacrament at home. Writing to Shenstone later, Holyoake describes how "nothing had been wanting, either to prolong her life or to prepare her for the other world" [16]. That his own wife, Mrs Davis, and Mr Outing, had been at her bedside throughout.

Henrietta was to die on 27 March 1756. Earlier that same month, her son and his wife had visited Edstone to see young Somervile, a short ride away, but did not bother to call. Now, however, the grieving household did not have long to wait. Lord Luxborough and his family were promptly on the scene, ostensibly to make arrangements for the funeral although it is clear that they really wanted to view the house.

In 1751, Henrietta had confided in Shenstone of her family's designs upon her home. How sad that she was right. In a matter of weeks his Lordship was to settle himself at Barrells where his behaviour was to be far from exemplary. Shenstone's response, although slow in coming was one of genuine sadness.

Nothing can alter the misery of Henrietta's final months – ameliorated only by the genuine love she inspired in her servants and neighbours. But now is the time to leave the grieving household and look, briefly into the future.

Chapter 16

AFTER HENRIETTA

Even Henrietta's remains did not rest in peace. As has been seen she died on 27 March 1757 and was buried at St Peter's Church, Wootton Wawen where her friend Lord Somervile was laid to rest. But not for long. Her coffin was later re-interred in a mausoleum on the Barrells' Estate – before being moved again to the Old Chapel, bordering the grounds,

The funeral took place on 5 April in the presence of church wardens Richard Baron and Lewis Bradley whose wife had been one of Henrietta's local friends. The register was signed by the then Curate-in-Charge, Oxford graduate George Hobday, but one would assume, unless his Lordship had deemed otherwise, that the service was conducted by her Ladyship's own Chaplain, William Holyoake.

In response to an enquiry from Shenstone, it was Holyoake who had written on March 29 to furnish the former with a more detailed account of her illness and death. Whether the poet attended her Ladyship's funeral is not known, for there is no mention of the occasion in his *Letters*, but if the entry under recorded deaths in *Gentleman's Magazine* for April 12, 1757 is anything to go by: "Lady Luxborough of Lord Luxborough of Ireland", it is reasonable to suppose that Henrietta's husband would not have encouraged many mourners.

What on the other hand we do know, is that within a matter of weeks Lord Luxborough had ensconced himself at Barrells where he was to install a series of mistresses and embark upon a life style which alternated between that of a country squire in Warwickshire and man-about-town in London, where he met the women he would keep away from prying eyes in the country. Things were quite different now as Shenstone was to impart to William Holyoake:

Oldberrow Church. Photograph, July 4 1891.

Eighteenth century map of Henley in Arden in Warwickshire, by William Yates.

Edstone Manor, home to Sir William Somervile.

The Leasowes, home to William Shenstone.

HENRIETTA'S GARDEN

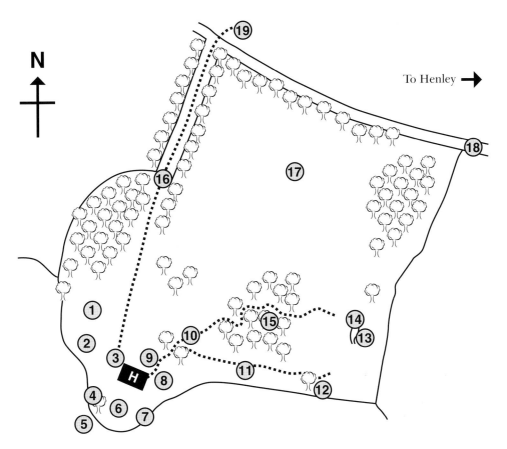

N

19

To Henley →

18

17

16

1

2

3

H

9

8

10

15

14

13

11

12

4

6

7

5

H = Probable location of house

1. Upper Garden
2. Bowling Green
3. Entrance Court
4. Grotto
5. Ha-Ha *(follows boundary)*
6. Lower Garden, Aviary and Fountain
7. Shrubbery
8. Kitchen Garden
9. Pheasant Yard
10. Lime Walk

11. Service Walk *(also contains shrubbery)*
12. Double-Oak Tree
13. Pit or Ravine
14. Hermitage
15. Coppice, with Abele Walk and Serpentine
16. The Long Walk, with *"27 good straight elms"*
17. Field/Meadow
18. Road to Henley
19. Path to Ullenhall Chapel

Diagram of the layout of Henrietta's garden, by Andrew Craythorne.

The famous Barrells' double oak. Photograph by Arthur Carden.

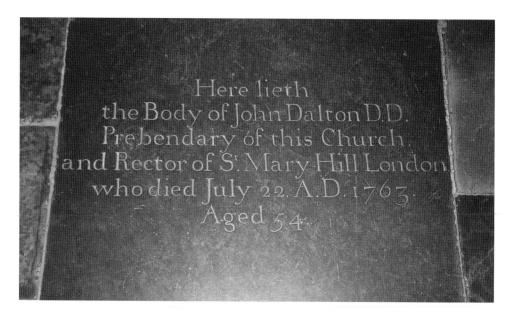

Here lieth
the Body of John Dalton D.D.
Prebendary of this Church,
and Rector of S.t Mary Hill London,
who died July 22. A.D. 1763.
Aged 54.

Memorial to John Dalton in crypt of Worcester Cathedral.

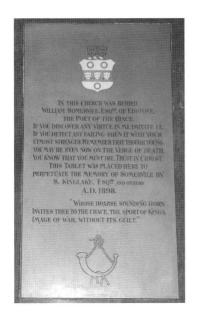

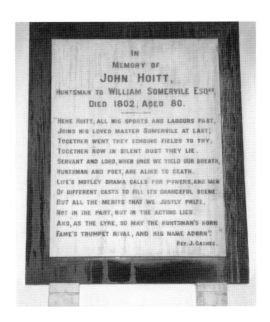

Left: Memorial to Sir William Somervile in Wootton Wawen Church.
Right: Plaque in memory of John Hoitt in Wootton Wawen Church.

Harbury Parish Church and "haunted" churchyard where Richard Jago was Rector.

Letter written in French by Henrietta to William Shenstone.

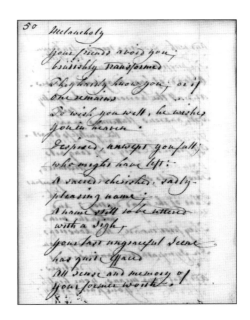

Left: Record of the marriage of Henrietta with John Knight.
Right: Extract from Robert Knight's commonplace-book.

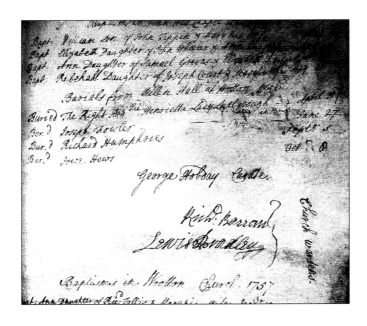

Record of Henrietta's burial, taken from Wootton Wawen Parish Register.

Ullenhall Chapel today, showing a commemorative plaque to members of the Knight family, including Henrietta (on the right hand side – see detail below).

Left: Letters of Administrations, June 1756. Right: Close up of right hand plaque.

...whatever may be now expended upon embellishments now at Barrells, it can hardly ever be, the agreeable object from your House that it had been [1].

Two months after his wife's death, Lord Luxborough married for a second time – with a Mrs Lequesne, the rich widow of a London alderman. It would appear that they never lived together, which poses a number of questions. Why did he marry her in the first place? Why was the marriage never annulled, an outcome which would later have left him free to marry again? The last we hear of Mrs Lequesne is that she was happily settled and living in Twickenham. What is to be made of this?

One thing is clear. After Mrs Lequesne, Lord Luxborough never again entertained the prospect of a third marriage. When in London, he was to live for some time at a brothel run by "Moll Clever Legs" who also acted for him as a procurer of young girls. Back at Barrells, it was from a selection of these that he chose his mistresses – one of whom, Miss Charlotte Day, was a woman with some taste as her predilection for auction rooms and valuable china demonstrates. No doubt it also caused problems for Lord Luxborough who, ever mindful of his money, was to replace her with Miss M...s from Vauxhall and land himself with another problem. He soon found himself obliged to lock her bedroom door to keep her from assignations with younger men – especially Sir Richard... whose appearance beneath her casement window one day was to encourage her to leap into his arms and out of Lord Luxborough's forever.

It was not until 1764 that Lord Luxborough met Jane Davies, the girl who was to become his common law wife; live with him at his London home in Golden Square and bear him five children. How they met is a story that could well belong to the realm of romantic fiction and is worth recounting. Jane's father, Farmer Davies, was the tenant of Moat Farm on the Barrells' Estate. He was experiencing financial difficulties, was unable to pay his rent, an obligation removed once Lord Luxborough caught sight of his modest and lovely daughter! The same daughter despatched to Barrells to offer a small sum – all that her father could afford in response to

Luxborough's request of the day before. But now the latter was predisposed to decline the money on condition that Jane would agree to come and live with him. The family accepted the offer and so did Jane who was, in fact, "sold" to settle her father's dues. And the outcome was a happy one. Miss Davis seems to have settled contentedly into her new role and one is reminded of Richard Graves, that member of Henrietta's Coterie who married Lucy.

When Lord Luxborough died, Jane changed her name by deed-poll in order that the children might carry on the family name and the eldest, a son, inherit the Barrells' Estate which first passed to Henry the son of Henrietta. Wootton Wawen Church is full of memorials to the Luxborough dynasty, including those children whose mother was Jane Davies.

All of which poses the question as to why Miss Davies succeeded in her relationship with Luxborough whilst Henrietta did not? The answer is likely to be that Jane posed no threat. She was not highly educated; had not dined with Pope, Bolingbroke or Arbuthnot; her expectations were altogether different. Lord Luxborough and Jane Davies were comfortable together in a way that he and Henrietta could never have been, for the latter's marriage was a misalliance – a mistake on a grand scale and one for which Henrietta was obliged to pay for the rest of her life.

Henrietta left behind many to mourn – for friendship to her was vital as food to the starving. The Holyoakes, husband and wife: Richard and Lucy Graves, the Jagos, her servants and many more. Finally there was Shenstone who had kept and collected her letters. An act which was to make possible their eventual publication by James Dodsley from originals in the possession of John Hodgetts, Shenstone's cousin and executor of his will. In a final act of remembrance, the poet had bound and inscribed the manuscripts with the following words:

Letters from the Right Honourable Lady Luxborough; written with abundant Ease, Politeness and Vivacity in which she was scarce equalled by any woman of her Time. They commenced in the year 1739 and were continued to the year of her death (1756) with some intermissions [2].

Shenstone's words are a fitting tribute to an interesting and determined woman. One who, as she herself says, had been forced to brave "the chequered chances of this life". Whose letters provide us with vivid glimpses into byways far from the bustle of town. Which tell of "rumpled" eggshells; of colliers as postmen; of water engines and thick gilt paper to write on.

Memories of Henrietta lived on in folk law – even into the nineteen forties. For it was then that a lady groom working on the Barrells' estate recounted her experiences. She would scent perfume and sense a benign "presence" as she carried out her duties in the old stable block which was originally part of the old house.

All is demolished now and only the lodge remains; a new house stands where once was Barrells Green. But Henrietta's sad story of bravery in adversity is still remembered by those sympathetic to her cause. Those who may well reflect upon the lot of women in the eighteenth century and be grateful that in modern times, less inequalities exist.

BIBLIOGRAPHY

BURMAN, John, *In The Forest of Arden*, (Birmingham, 1948).

BURMAN, John, *Warwickshire People and Places*, (Birmingham, 1936).

BURROWS, Donald, *Handel*, (Oxford, 1994).

CARDEN Arthur, E, (compiled) *The Knights of Barrells*. A scrapbook of documents and information; a limited edition, (Falmouth, 1993).

CLARENCE, Tracey, *A portrait of Richard Graves*, (Cambridge, 1987).

COOPER, William, *Henley in Arden*, (Cambridge, 1987).

COLLINS, John, Churton, *Bolingbroke; and Voltaire in England*, (London?, 1886).

COOPER, William, *Henley in Arden*, (Birmingham, 1946).

COOPER, William, *Wootton Wawen*, (Birmingham, 1936).

CRAYTHORNE, Andrew, *Barrells Hall: From Riches to Ruins*, (Birmingham, 2003).

DODSLEY, James, ed. *Letters Written by the Right Honourable Lady Luxborough to William Shenstone*, (London, 1775).

DODSLEY, James, William Shenstone's, *Essays on Men, Manners and Things*, Works Vol 2, (London, 1764).

DUGGAN, Audrey, *The World of William Shenstone*, (Studley, 2004).

FEENEY, Margaret, *Ullenhall – Life after Lady Luxborough*, (Studley, 1993).

GILFILLAN, Rev George, *William Shenstone's Poetical Works*, (Edinburgh, 1854).

HEY, G. Colin, *The Warwickshire Coterie*, (Stratford-upon-Avon, 1991).

HOPKINSON, M. R., *Married to Mercury*, (London, 1936).

HUGHES, Helen, S., *The Gentle Hertford*, (New York, 1940).

HULL, Thomas, ed. *Select Letters Between The Late Duchess of Somerset. William Shenstone and Others, Vols 1 and 2*, (London, 1778).

LINNANE, Fergus, *London's Underworld*, (London 2004).

LITTLE, Bryan, *Bath Portrait*, (Bristol, 1961).

MANGUS, J. J., *The King's Favour*, (Gloucestershire, 1991).

PICARD, Liza, *Dr Johnson's London*, (London 2000).

PORTER, Roy, *English Society in the Eighteenth Century*, (London, 1982).

QUENNELL, Peter, *Alexander Pope*, (London, 1968).

SICHEL, Walter, *Bolingbroke and his Times*, (London, 1902).

STIRLING, A. M. W., *Merry Wives of Battersea*, (London, 1956).

TREVELYAN, G. M, *English Social History*, (London, 1973).

TUBERVILE, A. S., *English Men and Manners in the Eighteenth Century*, (Oxford, 1926).

WHITEHOUSE, F. R. B., *Table Games of Georgian and Victorian Days*, (London, 1951).

WILLIAMS, Marjorie, ed., *The Letters of William Shenstone*, (Oxford, 1939).

WILLIAMS, Marjorie, ed., *Lady Luxborough Goes to Bath*, (Oxford 1946).

GENERAL REFERENCE

Alumni Oxoniensis, (Lichtenstein, 1968).

Aris' Gazette.

Burks Peerage.

Cambridge Guide to English Literature, (London, 1983).

Compton-Rickett, *History of English Literature*, (London, 1964).

Dictionary of National Geography.

Egmont Diaries.

Gentleman's Magazine.

Hutchinson's Encyclopaedia, (Oxford, 1994).

Lady Landover, ed. *Mrs Delany Autobiography and Correspondence*, Vol 2, (London, 1811).

Oxford Book of Quotations, (London, 1956).

Pevsner, Nikolaus, *London South*, (London 1973).

Pope, Alexander, *The Rape of the Lock,* (1712).

Shakespeare, William, *Hamlet,* (1602).

Smollett, Tobias, *Peregrine Pickle.* Introduction by Walter Allen, (London, 1967).

Wyndham, Maud, *Chronicles of the Eighteenth Century,* (London, 1924).

Young, E, and W., *London Churches,* (London 1956).

PERIODICALS, THESES, MANUSCRIPTS

Friends of Lydiard Tregoze, Report No 36.

Smith, Betty, *Focus,* Vol IV, No 8, Dec 1981/Jan 1982 pp 6-7.

Beatie, J. M. *The English Court in the Reign of George I,* (Cambridge, 1963).

Edge, Burnice, *Lady Luxborough and Her Circle,* (Birmingham, May 1930).

British Library, Add. Mss. 23728, Letters to Frances, Countess of Hertford.

British Library, Add. Mss. 45889, Letters to Bolingbroke, 1736-39.

British Library, Add. Mss. 34196, 57486, Letters to and from Bolingbroke 1718-37.

Lane, Joan, Manuscript Text, Library, Warwick University.

PERSONALIA

ALLEN, Ralph (1693–1764). Born Cornwall. Self-made man. Major employer Bath building-stone industry. At Prior Park from 1741. Centre of hospitality and culture. Entertained Henrietta 1752.

ALLEN, Rev. Thomas (-d.1753). Rector of Spernal. Close friend of Henrietta.

ARBUTHNOT, Dr John (1667–1735). Scottish writer and physician. Dedicatee of Pope's *Epistle to Dr Arbuthnot*. Creator of John Bull. Chief author *Memoirs of Martinus Scriblerus*. Friend of Pope, Swift, and Bolingbroke. Met Henrietta at Dawley, her brother's "farm".

ARCHER, Lord Thomas, First Baron Archer (1695–1768). Of Umberslade. Keen landscape gardener. Both neighbour and friend of Henrietta.

DALTON, Rev. John (1709–1763). Born Cumberland. Educated Queen's College, Oxford. MA, 1730. BD and DD 1750. Tutor to Frances Hertford's son, Viscount Beauchamp 1734. Met Henrietta at Marlborough 1734–1735. Cause of her exile to Barrells. Canon of Fifth Stall at Worcester Cathedral 1748. Also Rector St Mary-at-Hill, London. Died Worcester.

DEWS, Mrs John (1707–1761). Daughter of Bernard Granville. Younger sister to Mary, later Mrs Delaney. Discouraged Henrietta's overtures of friendship even though obliged to seek her help.

DOLMAN, Maria (1733–1754). Daughter of Reverend Thomas Dolman. Shenstone's cousin. Much admired by Henrietta. Died of smallpox contracted on holiday in London.

DODSLEY, Robert (1703–1764). Publisher, writer and bookseller. Rose from footman to fame with *Servitude*, a poem 1729. *The Toyshop*, a satirical play, 1730. Published Pope, Goldsmith, Johnson and Shenstone. Best known for his six volumes of *Miscellanies*, a Collection to which Henrietta contributed a number of her poems, Volume IV.

DUDLEY, Lord Fernando Dudley Lea. Fifth Baron. (-d.1759). Of the Grange, Lapal, Halesowen. Introduced Henrietta by Shenstone. Features frequently in her letters.

FIELDING, Henry (1707–1754). Popular eighteenth century novelist. Best known for *The History of Tom Jones*, 1749. *Joseph Andrews*, 1750. Justice of the Peace for Middlesex and Westminster 1748. Work much admired by Henrietta.

FIELDING, Sarah (1710–1768). Novelist sister to Henry. Best known for *The Adventures of David Simple* 1744. Also a sequel by the same name 1753. Met Henrietta at Prior Park 1752.

GAY, John (1685–1732). Poet and dramatist. Best known for *The Beggar's Opera* 1728. Satirised Walpole which led to the banning of *Polly*, a sequel. Met Henrietta at Dawley where he was a popular guest.

GRAVES, Rev. Richard (1715–1804). Poet, novelist and first biographer of William Shenstone met at Pembroke College, Oxford. Ordained 1740. Rector of Claverton near Bath. Novels include *Columella* and *The Spiritual Quixote*. Member Henrietta's Coterie.

HALL, Rev. Thomas (c1713–??). Educated Solihull School. Rector of Beaudesert, Henley-in-Arden. Friend and contemporary of Shenstone. Friend of Henrietta. Obtained 1749 additional living of Harborough Magna, near Rugby.

HANDEL, George, Frideric (1685–1759). Foremost German composer and organist. Resident in England from 1711. Composed operas and dramatic oratorios, including *Messiah* (1747). Awarded an annual pension of £600 by George I. Friend of Henrietta.

JAGO, Rev. Richard (1715–1781). Son Rector of Beaudesert, Henley-in-Arden. Educated Solihull School and Oxford. Minor poet. Published 1759, *Edgehill*. Contributor to Dodsley's *Miscellany*. Rector of Harbury in Warwickshire. Member of Henrietta's Coterie.

KNIGHT, Robert, Baron Luxborough, Earl of Catherlough (1702–1772). Estranged husband of Henrietta. Son of cashier of South Sea Bubble

Company. After a second marriage (unconsummated) to Lady de
Quesne 1756, took as his common law wife Jane Davies, daughter of a
tenant. By her fathered five children.

LYTTELTON, Sir George of Hagley Hall. First Baron (1709–1773).
Educated Eton and Oxford. Entered Parliament 1735. Minor poet.
Generous patron. Friend of Shenstone through whom he met Henrietta.

MEREDITH, Amos (-d.1744). Married Henrietta's first cousin, Johanna
Cholmondley. His wife and two daughters, including the thespian, Miss
Patty, frequent visitors to Barrells.

NASH, Richard (Beau Nash) (1674–1761). Born Swansea. Educated
Carmarthen Grammar School and Jesus College, Oxford. Brief army
career. Superb self-publicist. Master of Ceremonies, Bath, 1705–1761.
Regulated anti-social behaviour. Authoritarian figure. His white beaver
hat a symbol of office described by Henrietta in letter to Shenstone.

NEEDHAM, Mother. Well known brothel keeper. Represented in first
episode of Hogarth's *Harlot's Progress*. Convicted 1731, of keeping a
disorderly house. Sentenced to the pillory where "pelted in an
unmerciful manner", she soon died.

PETERS, Dr Charles (1695–1746). Respected London medical practitioner.
Physician Extraordinary to King George II, (1743). Physician St
George's Hospital, London from 1735.

POPE, Alexander (1688–1744). English poet and satirist. Precocious talent.
Best known for his parody of the heroic couplet in *The Rape of the Lock*
1712–14. Translator of Homer's *Illiad* and *Odyssey* 1714 and 1726. *The
Dunciad* 1728, a satire on scholarly dullness – and much more. Met
Henrietta at Dawley.

RICHARDSON, Samuel (1689–1761). Sensationally popular novelist.
Printer to House of Commons. Published *Pamela 1740–41,* a novel in
the form of letters. Clarissa 1747–8. Brother-in-law to Mr Leake of
Leake's book shop in Bath. Met Henrietta at Prior Park. Features in her
letters to Shenstone.

ROWE, Elizabeth, née Singer (1674–1737). Daughter of Walter Singer, a
non-conformist minister. Began writing at twelve. Under nom de plume

Philomena, contributed verses to *Athenium Mercury.* Published *Poems on Several Occasions 1696.* Widowed 1715. Her lines *On the Death of Thomas Rowe,* appended by Pope to second edition of his *Eloise to Abelard.* Met Henrietta at Marlborough.

ST JOHN, The Honourable George (1693–1716). Henrietta's brother. Appointed British Ambassador extraordinary and plenipotentiary to Italian States 1711. On hand during negotiations over Treaty of Utrecht. Which he brought back to London.

ST JOHN, Sir Henry, Fourth Baronet (1652–1742). Henrietta's roué father. Convicted murder Sir Edward Estcourt 1689. Reprieved gallows after payment of bribe. Fled to France. Upon return, created Viscount St John of Battersea 1716.

ST JOHN, The Honourable Hollis (1710–1738). Youngest of Henrietta's three brothers. Fourth equerry Queen Caroline 1736. His will left Henrietta family jewels, a farm at Peckham Rye and shares in Covent Garden Theatre. Despised by his half-brother, Henry Bolingbroke.

ST JOHN, The Honourable Henry (1678–1751). Created Viscount Bolingbroke 1713. Henrietta's influential half-brother. British Tory politician and political philosopher. Foreign Secretary 1710–1714. Negotiated Treaty of Utrecht 1713. Jacobite conspirator. Fled France. Returned to England 1725. Settled Dawley. His *Idea of a Patriot King* 1738 and *Dissertation upon Parties,* laid foundation nineteenth century Toryism.

SHENSTONE, Joseph (1722–1751). Younger brother of William. Trained as attorney in Bridgenorth but never practised. Repeatedly ill. Lived with William at the Leasowes. Much liked by Henrietta.

SHENSTONE, William (1714–1763). Midland poet and gentleman of letters. Much sought after as landscape gardener. Best known for *The Schoolmistress* 1739, revised 1742 – amusing account of his days at Sarah Lloyd's dame school. Aided Dodsley with editing his *Miscellanies.* Contributed numerous poems to Volume IV. Great friend of Henrietta. Entertained her frequently at his home, The Leasowes, in Halesowen.

SMOLLET, Tobias, George (1721–1771). Author of *Roderick Random* 1748 *Peregrine Pickle 1751*. Incorporates as Chapter 88, notorious *Memoirs* of Lady Vane known to youthful Henrietta.

SOAMES, Sir Peter. Second cousin to Henrietta. Great grandson Sir Walter St John. Frequent visitor to Barrells.

SOMERVILE, William, Sir (1675–1742). Warwickshire poet and country squire of Edstone near Henley-in-Arden. Educated Winchester and New College Oxford. Published *The Chase* 1735, a poem in blank verse concerned with field sports. *Hobbinol,* 1740, a mock heroic account of rustic May Games in Vale of Evesham. Friend of Henrietta and early member of her Coterie.

THYNNE, Frances, Countess of Hertford (1699–1754). Married Algernon Seymour, Earl of Hertford 1715. Duchess of Somerset 1748. Literary hostess, poet and correspondent. Patroness of Stephen Duck the "thresher poet" and James Thomson, author of *The Seasons*. Loyal friend to Henrietta.

VANE, Viscountess Frances, Anne. Née Hawes (c.1713–1788). Her Memoirs, "the bad story of a wicked woman" appeared as Chapter 88 in Smollet's *Peregrine Pickle*. Shocked Henrietta and contemporary society.

De Villette, The Marquise Marie Claire (1675–1750). Née Deschamps de Marcilly. Brought up Court in Louis XIV. Second wife of Henry Bolingbroke 1722. Well liked by Henrietta.

WHARTON, Angelica, Magdalena (1666–1736). Née Pellissary. Henrietta's mother. Married Lord St John, as a young widow 1686. Allegedly died heart-broken after Henrietta's "disgrace".

WHISTLER, Anthony (1714–1754). Born Whitchurch, Berkshire. Educated Eton and Oxford. Lifelong friend William Shenstone. Author of *The Shuttlecock*, a mock heroic poem. Pleased Henrietta. Member of the Coterie.

WINCHCOMBE, Frances (1679–1718). Daughter of Sir Henry Winchcombe, Second Baronet of Bucklebury. Married The Hon. Henry St John 1701. A misalliance which destroyed her health.

LIST OF ILLUSTRATIONS

The Hon. Henrietta Knight, Henrietta's daughter. Attributed to Joseph Highmore. By kind permission of Mrs D P Johnson.

The Hon. Henry Knight, Henrietta's son. Attributed to Joseph Highmore. By kind permission of Mrs D P Johnson.

Frances Thynne, Lady Hertford, later Duchess of Somerset. Attributed to Thomas Hudson. By kind permission of the Duke of Northumberland and courtesy of The Courtauld Institute of Art – Alnwick Collection.

Elizabeth Rowe. Artist unknown. Courtesy of Birmingham Library Services.

A view of Battersea c.1750. From an engraving for the Royal Magazine. Courtesy of Wandsworth Local History Library.

Bolingbroke House (Battersea Manor). From an original woodcut. Date unknown. Courtesy of Wandsworth Local History Library.

The Cedar Room, Battersea Manor. From a photograph c.1911. Courtesy of Wandsworth Local History Library.

Ceiling of Cedar Room, illustrating delicate strapwork plaster. From a photograph c.1911. Plasterwork Ceiling, Battersea Manor. Courtesy of Wandsworth Local History Library.

Gallery Two

The Rotunda, Ranelagh Gardens by Canaletto. Courtesy of The National Gallery, London.

Detail of a map from The A to Z of Georgian London, by John Rocque, c.1746. Courtesy of Birmingham Library Services.

Alexander Pope, by William Hoare. Courtesy of the National Portrait Gallery, London.

John Gay, by William Aikman c.1729. Courtesy of the National Portrait Gallery, London.

George Frideric Handel, by William Bromley; Thomas Hudson. Courtesy of the National Portrait Gallery, London.

Ralph Allen, by John Faber Junior; Thomas Hudson. Courtesy of the National Portrait Gallery, London.

Samuel Richardson, by Joseph Highmore. Courtesy of the National Portrait Gallery, London.

Henry Fielding, by William Hogarth. Courtesy of National Portrait
  Gallery, London.
William Shenstone, by Edward Alcock. Courtesy of National Portrait
  Gallery, London.
William Somervile, artist unknown. Courtesy of National Portrait Gallery,
  London.
Richard Graves, by Samuel William Reynolds, from an engraving by
  James Northcote. Courtesy of National Portrait Gallery, London.
Richard (Beau) Nash, artist unknown. Courtesy of the National Portrait
  Gallery, London.
Spernal Church and Parsonage. Drawing by James Saunders, c.1810.
  Courtesy of The Shakespeare Birthplace Trust.
Ullenhall Chapel. Drawing by James Saunders, c.1810. Courtesy of The
  Shakespeare Birthplace Trust.
Beaudesert Church. Drawing by James Saunders, c.1810. Courtesy of
  The Shakespeare Birthplace Trust.

Gallery Three
Oldberrow Church. Photograph, July 4 1891. Contributed by Edwin C.
  Middleton. Courtesy of Birmingham Library Services.
Eighteenth century map of Henley in Arden in Warwickshire, by William
  Yates. Courtesy of Birmingham Library Services.
Edstone Manor, home to Sir William Somervile. Courtesy of Birmingham
  Library Services.
The Leasowes, home to William Shenstone. From an original drawing by
  William Shenstone in the possession of the author.
Diagram of the layout of Henrietta's garden, by Andrew Craythorne. By
  kind permission of Mr John Craythorne.
The famous Barrells' double oak. Photograph by Arthur Carden. By kind
  permission of Arthur Carden.
Memorial to John Dalton in crypt of Worcester Cathedral. Photograph by
  Geoffrey Duggan.

Memorial to Sir William Somervile in Wootton Wawen Church. Photograph by Geoffrey Duggan.

Plaque in memory of John Hoitt in Wootton Wawen Church. Photograph by Geoffrey Duggan.

Harbury Parish Church and "haunted" churchyard where Richard Jago was Rector. Photograph by Geoffrey Duggan.

Letter written in French by Henrietta to William Shenstone, Courtesy of The Shakespeare Birthplace Trust.

Record of the marriage of Henrietta with John Knight. Courtesy of Westminster Record Office.

Extract from Robert Knight's commonplace-book. By kind permission of Arthur Carden.

Record of Henrietta's burial, taken from Wootton Wawen Parish Register. Courtesy of Worcester Records Office.

Ullenhall Chapel today, showing a commemorative plaque to members of the Knight family, including Henrietta. Photograph by Geoffrey Duggan.

Letters of Administrations, June 1756. Courtesy of the National Archives, Kew.

Close up of right hand memorial plaque in Ullenhall Chapel. Photograph by Geoffrey Duggan.

APPENDIX

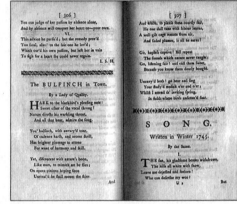

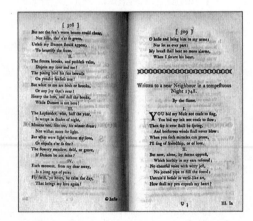

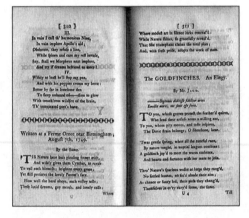

Taken from Vol. IV of Dodsley's Miscellanies.

REFERENCES

1. Birth and Background

1   Website: The Church of Jesus Christ of Latter-day Saints

2   Linnade, p.219

3   Hopkinson, p.75

4   Porter, p.39

5   Stirling, p.27

6   Hopkinson, p.210

7   Compton-Rickett, p.202

8   Stirling, p.34

9   Blake, *Songs of Innocence and Experience*, p.5

10 Stirling, p.27

2. The Young Henrietta

1   Porter, p.39

2   Ibid., p.38

3   Boswell I, p.463

4   Whitehouse, p ?

5   Sichel, p.511

6   Delaney I, p.16

7   Ibid., p.147

8   Hull I, p.16

9   Ibid., p.67

10 Pope *Rape*, Canto III

11 Compton Rickett, p.206

12 Letter to Martha Blount

13 Sichel, p.500

14 Ibid., p.500, Note 4

15 Sichel, p.483

16 Hughes, p.13

17 Sichel, p.494

18 Hopkinson, p.23

3. Friendship

1   Hughes, p.27

2   Ibid., p.23

3   Ibid., p.431

4   Guarini, *Canto IV*

4. Marriage

1   Hughes, p.127

2   Ibid., p.128

3   Ibid., p.133

4   Sichel, p.493

5   Carden, p.40

6   Sichel, p.517

7   Ibid., p.518

8   Hopkinson, p.43

9   Sichel, p.522
10   Hughes, p.122
11   Sichel, p 530
12   Hughes, p.135
13   Ibid., p.171
14   Ibid., p.171
15   Ibid., p.181

5.   Scandal
1   Carden, p.102
2   Sichel, p.473
3   Report 14 HMC 1896.
     Quoting from "Anecdotes
     and Other Miscellaneous
     Pieces"; left by the Right
     Honourable Arthur Onslow
4   Stirling, p.43
5   Ibid., p.44
6   Ibid., p.44
7   Sichel, p.549
8   Ibid., p.140, Note 2
9   Stirling, p.46
10   Ibid., p.47
11   Commonplace-book p.39
12   The agreement was to
     prohibit her from
     approaching within 20
     miles of London on the Bath
     Road
13   Stirling, p.45
14   Ibid., p.46
15   Ibid., p.45

6.   Exile
1   Marshal, *Report 36*, p.16
2   Carden, p.107
3   Marshal, *Report 36*, p.16
4   Luxborough, p.40
5   Ibid., p.41
6   Ibid., p.41
7   Ibid., p.58
8   Williams (ed.), p.233

7.   The Coterie
1   Luxborough, p.1
2   Ibid., p.2
3   Jago, *Edgehill III*, p.101
4   Somervile, *The Chase*, Canto I
5   Gilfillan (ed.), p.173
6   Chambers (ed.), XVII, p.313
7   Dodsley (ed.) IV, p.329
8   Luxborough, p.19
9   Williams (ed.), p.140
10   Carden, p.36
11   Gilfillan (ed.), p.184
12   Chambers XVII, p.310
13   Luxborough, p.2
14   Marshall, *Report 36*, p.21
15   Williams (ed.), p.56
16   From a plaque in Wootton
     Wawen Church,
     Warwickshire
17   British Library, ADD MS.
     45889 ff 62
18   Carden, p.142

8. The Wider Circle

1 *Gentleman's Magazine*, May 1798
2 Williams (ed.), p.385
3 Luxborough, p.356
4 Hull, Vol.4, p.140
5 Luxborough, p.170
6 Hutton, p.165
7 Delaney, Vol II, first series, p.586
8 Delaney, Vol II, first series, p.578
9 Williams (ed.), p.44

9. Barrells House and Garden

1 Marshall, *Report 36*, p.15
2 Ibid., p.15
3 Ibid., p.15
4 Luxborough, p.27
5 Ibid., p.27
6 Ibid., p.65
7 Ibid., p.6
8 Duggan, p.73
9 Marshal, *Report 36*, p.21
10 Williams (ed.), p.136
11 Luxborough, p.22
12 Ibid., p.22
13 Ibid., p.16
14 Williams (ed.), p.338
15 Ibid., p.230
16 Duggan, p.59
17 Luxborough, p.90
18 Marshall, *Report 36*, p.21
19 Luxborough, p.15
20 British Library Ms 45889
21 Luxborough, p.97
22 Ibid., p.121
23 Ibid., p.116
24 Ibid., p.38
25 Ibid., p.90
26 Ibid., p.95
27 Ibid., p.97
28 Williams (ed.), p.109
29 Luxborough, p.100
30 Ibid., p.100
31 Williams (ed.), p.285
32 Luxborough, p.202
33 Gilfillan, p.273
34 Williams (ed.), p.202
35 Luxborough, p.92
36 Ibid., p.252
37 Ibid., p.252
38 Luxborough, p.62
39 Luxborough, p.131
40 Ibid., p.134
41 Ibid., p.131
42 Williams (ed.), p.14
43 Luxborough, p.193
44 Williams (ed.) p.198
45 Marshall, *Report 37*, p ?
46 Luxborough, p.355

10. Lady Luxborough's Letters to William Shenstone

1 Luxborough, p.9
2 Ibid., p.61
3 Ibid., p.206

4   Ibid., p.106

5   Ibid., p.184

6   Williams (ed.), p.109

7   Luxborough, p.82

8   Ibid., p.70

9   Ibid., p.64

10   Ibid., p.370

11   Ibid., p.277

12   Shenstone *Works Vol I*, p.135

13   Luxborough, p.162

14   Ibid., p.282

15   Ibid., p.285

16   Ibid., p.283

17   Williams (ed.), p.316

18   Luxborough, p.295

19   Williams (ed.), p.448

20   Luxborough, p.111

21   Ibid., p.82

22   Ibid., p.160

23   Ibid., p.161

24   Ibid., p.304

25   Ibid., p.304

26   Williams (ed.), p.140

27   Luxborough, p.88

28   Ibid., p.266

29   Ibid., p.21

30   Williams (ed.), p.139

31   Luxborough, p.293

32   Ibid., p.20

33   Ibid., p.55

34   Ibid., p.36

35   Ibid., p.12

11. My Brother Bolingbroke

1   Collins, p.1

2   Hopkinson, p.75

3   Ibid., p.113

4   Quennell, p.60

5   Shenstone *Works Vol II*, p.279

6   Hill, *Vol II*, p.184

7   Hopkinson, p.20

8   Sichel, p.530

9   Marshall, *Report 36*, p.17

10   Ibid., p.17

11   Hopkinson, p.210

12   Ibid., p.221

13   Ibid., p.171

14   Ibid., p.226

15   Ibid., p.227

16   Ibid., p.228

17   Ibid., p.229

18   Luxborough, p.262

19   Ibid., p.285

20   Hopkinson, p.231

21   Luxborough, p.287

22   Ibid., p.287

23   Luxborough, p.287

12. Literary Interests

1   Williams (ed.), p.50

2   Luxborough, p.3

3   Gilfillan (ed.), p.139

4   Luxborough, p.25

5   Gilfillan (ed.), p.277

6   Luxborough, p.119

7   Williams (ed.), p.144

8   Ibid., p.175

9   Luxborough, p.62

10 Ibid., p.64

11 Ibid., p.68

12 Williams (ed.), p.181

13 Luxborough, p.80

14 Shenstone *Works, Vol I*, p.7

15 Luxborough, p.361

16 Williams (ed.), p.421

17 Luxborough, p.401

18 Williams (ed.), p.429

13. Henrietta's Poetry

1   Hughes, p.171

2   Dodsley (ed.), *Miscellanies,* Vol IV, p.309

3   Ibid., p.307

4   Ibid., p.306

5   Gilfillan (ed.), p.169

6   Luxborough, p.279

7   Dodsley (ed), *Miscellanies,* Vol IV, p.306

8   Luxborough, p.34

14. Henrietta's Visit to Bath

1   Williams, *Bath,* pp.20–21

2   Luxborough, p.297

3   Ibid., p.292

4   Williams, *Bath,* pp.14–15

5   Ibid., p.19

6   Ibid., p.19

7   Ibid., p.24

8   Ibid., p.24

9   Ibid., p.31

10 Luxborough, p.296

11 Ibid., p.296

12 Ibid., p.298

13 Ibid., p.298

14 Ibid., p.49

15. The Return Home

1   Luxborough, p.306

2   Ibid., p.313

3   Ibid., p.310

4   Ibid., pp.310–311

5   Ibid., p.393

6   Ibid., p.394

7   Ibid., p.325

8   Hull (ed.), *Vol I*, p.151

9   Luxborough, p.344

10 Ibid., p.347

11 Ibid., p.354

12 Gilfillan (ed.), p.177

13 Luxborough, p.411

14 Ibid., p.410

15 Williams (ed.), p.449

16 Luxborough, p.115

16. After Henrietta

1   Williams (ed.), p.453

2   Luxborough, p.iv

INDEX

BY THE SAME AUTHOR

Rhyme on the Spray – Collected Verse

A Sense of Occasion – Mendelssohn in Birmingham

A Lady of Letters – A Biography of Catherine Hutton

The World of William Shenstone – A Biography of William Shenstone